Almost There

ALSO BY NUALA O'FAOLAIN

Are You Somebody? The Accidental Memoir of a Dublin Woman

My Dream of You

NUALA O'FAOLAIN

Almost There

THE ONWARD JOURNEY OF A DUBLIN WOMAN

RIVERHEAD BOOKS

NEW YORK

2003

RIVERHEAD BOOKS
A member of
Penguin Putnam Inc.
375 Hudson Street
New York, NY 10014

Library of Congress Cataloging-in-Publication Data

O'Faolain, Nuala.
Almost there : the onward journey of a Dublin woman / Nuala
O'Faolain.
p.   cm.
ISBN 1-57322-241-0
1. O'Faolain, Nuala.   2. Journalists—Ireland—Biography.
I. Title.
PN5146.O39 A3   2003   2002036722
070.92—dc21
[B]

Printed in the United States of America
10   9   8   7   6   5   4   3   2   1

Book design by Marysarah Quinn

For my dear sister, Deirdre

Almost There

CHAPTER ONE

The Low Point

IF I HAD BEEN ASKED TO REPORT ON middle age when I was halfway through my fifties, I would have said that it was too bleak to talk about. Much too bleak if you believed, as I passionately did, that your life has been a failure. I seemed successful, I knew—I was an opinion columnist with an Irish newspaper, and columnists are not nobodies. But when I looked at the private side of my life, all I could feel was regret, and all I could see was what was missing. I had no child, and no other creation. I didn't have a partner. I didn't have a lover, however provisional, and I didn't have any appetite for one. I occasionally saw my sisters and brothers who lived near me, but I didn't think of them as a resource for everyday living. Our father had been a big fish in a small pond because he was the first journalist in Dublin to write a daily social diary about the receptions and parties and formal events that happened around the town every night. His dapper, charming figure, usually wearing evening dress, had been welcome everywhere he went. Not so, my poor mother. She was a shy, lonely woman, the inefficient manageress of wherever we happened to be living, a bookworm who, when she added drinking to reading, could escape the reality of nine children and a husband she was in love with but could not trust. Over the years, we watched our father become more sought after and our mother become a hopeless alcoholic. Worry about her became a bond between us when she was left a widow, but once she died too, the family didn't seem to have any function. Anyway, I felt that at the age of fifty-five I shouldn't be depending on the family I came from; I should have made a circle of my own. As it was, I didn't even have the company of colleagues in a workplace because I wrote my columns from home. And the truth was that I made no effort to find company. Every night I quietly drank just a bit too much wine, and other people would have interfered with that. There were only ten years to go till retirement from the paper. But what would I retire for? I had no savings, and because I'd only just joined the staff I wasn't going to have much of a pension. I had no plans anyway. My job with *The Irish Times* was much the best thing I had.

There's a famous challenge for writers in creating a character who's a convincing bore without boring the reader—

Shakespeare is said to have pulled it off with the Nurse in *Romeo and Juliet*. I was so dull back then that even a description of my dullness would have too much life in it. I don't know that anyone outside me looked closely enough to know how I felt, but I was so low I thought I'd never come back up. When you're young, the endings of relationships are all swirling feeling, and the practical implications don't matter. But it's different when you're a shade nearer sixty than fifty, and you had taken it for granted that what you had together would be your life to the end. The house, with its dustmarks and jangling hangers where her clothes had been, was a constant reminder of the breakup with a woman so well known in Ireland as an activist and writer that she is a household name: Nell. Our home had also been an office for professional work, so there was all that to sort out—the telephones and the cable companies and the shared expenditures and the rerouting of mail. There were dishes, plants, quilts. Things reappeared. The porcelain soup tureen we bought that day in eastern Hungary when we saw Russia in the distance—a dark forestry plantation on the other side of a river—and sang "Lara's Theme" at the top of our lungs to whoever might be over there. Things like that, carrying our history, now devalued. And what about friends, holidays, the two families, all that we knew about each other and had allowed to be known? The house became more silent every day as her departure drained the life from it.

But I read once that certain pine trees need extreme cold to germinate—that is, the cold of the worst of winter starts new life in them by splitting their seeds. At least now, the wrangling was over. There were still strong bonds between us, and on my side gratitude, but I've seen it happen to other couples, too, that every sentence becomes a flashpoint, every statement is disputed, every point is hung on to until one person proves that the other is wrong. Dry, angry victories. We went for a kind of marriage guidance to a psychologist friend. After nine sessions she said to us, "Couldn't you go on living in the same house but make it an absolute rule not to talk to each other at all or have anything whatsoever to do with each other?" I read my book from six o'clock every evening in my room, my bottle of wine beside me. Nell worked in her own room. We would share a tight-lipped meal, cooked by me. She would not say thank you because she felt silently pressured into it. I would flame with silent rage because she did not say thank you. And one day, the previously unimaginable became possible. I had never even in my most secret thoughts imagined us parting, but suddenly it was the only thing we could do. She had harried me on some point—I used to back away from the sound of her voice—down the hallway as far as the front door. I leaned against it, turned around, and said the sentences that begin, "Just go!"

And that was that, after almost fifteen years.

I don't know of any other event that causes as much pain and destruction, and that is as little understood, as the end of love. It's written off as a woman's thing, as if men don't suffer just as much—financially, often, more—when a relationship breaks down. What authenticity is it that people are honoring when they refuse to live under the same roof—even roofs as wide as, say, the mansions Charles and Diana had at their disposal—though the well-being of children depends on it, though businesses depend on it, though everything is as it was except that the tide of affection has gone out? And why, when it does go out, can nothing at all make it come in again? For nothing that a name can be put to, the whole world of a shared life is torn into pieces and the pieces scattered, as if truth depended on getting rid of it. Maybe it was an illusion in the first place, the love, but if so, why should its absence be so devastating? What is it, anyway, within oneself, that is hurt so much by a withdrawal nobody wanted to happen and nobody can control?

When the tide went out for us I saw in the sand, so to speak, the outline of my obdurate self, which the years of companionship had obscured. It seemed to me proved, now, that I could not sustain a loving relationship. I had no experience of anything other than love disappearing, however long that took. It had been like that from the beginning: the first man I ever adored was the first man I left. This was a man in whose arms I had learned what making love can be

like, a man with whom I'd seen the Mediterranean for the
first time, who'd played Mozart on his old cottage piano for
me, who'd slept out in the open with me and woken me to
marvel at a satellite going across the indigo sky through the
tracery of the cherry tree overhead. He had faithfully waited
at piers and in train stations for me, shopped and cooked for
me, bought things for me—sandals, I remember, elegant
little sandals with fine red straps and a kitten heel, in San
Remo—and yet I stood on a street in Dublin one winter
night and he stood in front of me trying to talk, and I was
surreptitiously rocking on one foot while I dangled the
other one in the gutter. Barely, barely moving, concentrat-
ing on the tiny, inward feel of the rocking, so as to pass the
time till he would stop talking and to distract myself from
listening to him. And he had done nothing and I had done
nothing to bring this about, nor was it in his interest or
mine. It was just pure waste. And then much the same happened with the next person I greatly loved, except that this
time he left me, and now this, the one that was meant to last
forever. Gone.

But I had blessings to count. Though the house was
lonely, the loneliness was purely private. I had my public
role: I might easily hear something I'd written in the newspaper quoted on radio or television, or I myself would be on
a discussion program. I valued my job very highly, not just
the privilege of working out my point of view in front of an

audience once a week, but the pleasure of finding the words for the arguments. The column wasn't very well paid, but then, I didn't work very hard. With what I had, I was paying off the mortgages on the Dublin house and on a two-room cottage in the west of Ireland. The Dublin house wasn't a home anymore, and the Clare one wasn't one yet—it had no heating, for one thing, and nothing to cook on except a broken range—but I loved being there. Whether in the west or in Dublin, I read all the time—the summer of the breakup I finished *Remembrance of Things Past* for the second time.

The hours of the evening when I listened to classical music and read with my whole self were rich. People think that solitary drinkers are fighting off misery, but it isn't like that—if anything, it's too attractive an occupation. And although I did drink too much I was still drinking less than I did in my thirties and forties. I honestly considered myself rather disciplined about drinking—when you have an alcoholic mother, almost anything short of gross alcoholism feels like an achievement. I was in good health anyway—"thank God" comes involuntarily to my lips when I say that, not because I think that there is a god who knows about me, but because I know that if you're not fortunate enough to be physically and mentally well, there's not much you can do about anything else. I was healthier, in fact, than I'd been since I was a girl, since I had managed that year, with incredible difficulty, to give up smoking cigarettes. This may seem a small thing, but anyone who has ever been a chain-smoker like me will know that quitting is so hard that you can hardly believe it—you move around delicately because your head feels as if it might fall off, and also because you're stunned at what you're trying to do. Conquering the addiction had been an action on the philosophic level, as well as every other. It involved taking hold of the way I imagined time. Instead of picturing the days stretching endlessly ahead, intolerably cigaretteless, I managed to train part of my mind into being in the here and now, where I could make the repeated decision not to smoke.

But I was barely succeeding. I followed people who were smoking in the street to gulp their slipstreams. In cafés and trains I was a keen passive smoker. I was obsessed with having cigarettes in my pocket to finger, so for months I carried a full pack in my pocket, replacing it with another when it became battered and began to leak tobacco. Once, a perfect stranger ran into a store after me and grabbed me to stop me buying the replacement pack, because he, like half of Ireland, had read my articles about trying to quit.

"I carry the pack so I won't feel deprived," I explained desperately. "The important thing is to avoid awakening every bit of deprivation you ever had in your life, beginning with the loss of the maternal breast. You have to emphasize to yourself that quitting is not a thing that's been done to you but a choice you've made."

He looked dubious. I didn't blame him. I was trying to brainwash myself into believing what the woman who ran the stop-smoking clinic had said. But I didn't believe anything she said. I didn't believe anything I said myself. I didn't believe anything except that I had a gaping void within me that ached to be filled full of smoke.

And yet—I did not fail. I became an ex-smoker. And after that I was able to believe in myself along a wider front. I decided to get a laptop computer and learn how to use it to send my pieces of journalism to the paper. So, after years of making no effort to learn anything new, I learned that. The laptop's Delete function was so different from the old typewritten sheets with their rows of Xs—reminders of each word and phrase that had been laboriously thought better of—that language itself seemed a refreshed medium now. Words swam into their place, where before they were cemented in.

I also decided to get a dog. And that's what I did, just before things went finally wrong in the relationship with Nell—indeed, I've wondered if my unconscious knew she and I were going to part and prompted me to get the dog so as to have something to keep my heart alive. I got Molly from the animal pound, a black and white mostly sheepdog mongrel pup, and I took her home and followed her around the house with wads of newspaper. I got her in advance of loving her. I had no idea of the abundance of pristine love a dog can release. I had no idea how grateful I was going to feel to her just for living with me. She was—she is—an honest, trusting, anxious little enthusiast of a dog, and I watched her as if I could learn from her—as if the simple truth she lives in is something a human can learn. And then I got a big, glossy, black cat, to keep Molly company. Not a very lovable cat, Hodge, but an impressive one, and above all, beautiful.

IT TOOK A WHILE to dismantle the home we'd shared and for Nell to move out, so I borrowed a place for myself, a former farmhouse in the foothills above Dublin full of big, creaking wardrobes and imitation board walls and brown linoleum laid on the uneven floor. The heavy furniture—sideboards, carved dining-room chairs—had no connection with comfort, and there was nowhere to sit outside except among ragged fruit bushes that sheltered behind a privet hedge in knee-high grass. I was nervous about the house's noises at night. She had always been the brave one. Near the house, along the base of the hill, a suburb was encroaching, with bungalows still raw with unpainted plaster standing on the rutted earth the builders left behind, bright children's swings already erect where the lawn would be. But an ancient lane led upward between banks thick with hawthorn. A pair of weathered gate-piers marooned in the middle of a field showed that once there had been a culti-vated estate here, where now the hillside waited to be turned into sites for houses. I used to walk with Molly across the springy turf and in and out of the groves of scrub oak. And one evening at the very end of that summer—the trees beginning to weep leaves—I lost her. I called and called along the hill, but no little black figure came bound-ing toward me.

The panic was over in an hour, when she broke, panting, through the old raspberry bushes behind the house to push her muzzle into my hand. But in that hour, I'd come as near to total breakdown as ever in my life. I was so stricken at the thought of losing Molly that I shouted out loud, hurrying down the lane and then past whatever people there were in the bungalows and then along the side of the main road, oblivious of the traffic. I was streaming with tears and talk-ing to myself: "No! No! No!" I think I meant that I would not accept that the dog was gone—I would not accept that, and I would not accept any more of anything bad, any loss, any grief. I had had enough. And at the same time I was praying out loud, "Let her be there, let her come back, let her be all right, please, please God . . ." I am embarrassed, writing this, to remember how crazy I must have seemed, and how close to crazy I really was, when thinking I'd lost the dog woke up too vividly everything I'd ever lost—my mother and father, all the other people, all the love affairs, all the places I'd lived, all the intimacy and warmth of my home, the investment of all the years of love that came to nothing. Everything.

I WRITE THIS six years later. I'm in America, in a half-forgotten part of New York State about three hours north-west of Manhattan, a gentle district of wooded hills and small lakes and plain villages, near the Delaware River. I'm sitting at the kitchen table, which is the only table in an apartment as spartan as a student dormitory, on the top floor of a shabby wooden house, one of a number of houses shaded by huge old pine trees on a sloping hillside above a lake. It's early in the morning and a golden light strikes in through the window thickly screened against summer bugs. Soon the sultry sun of August will heat the air. The old, gray dog who is living with me—Mimmo—who sleeps a lot of the time, will begin to wriggle with discomfort, and I'll walk him down the grass and over the road to the plank jetty, and he'll cool himself for a minute at the edge of the lake and when he settles to his keen inspection of the bees in the bushes of purple loosestrife I'll disturb the transpar-ent fish by sliding into the soft water myself. Odd, that in the novel I wrote during the last few years, the heroine, who is also looking after someone else's dog, swims in a lake with brown water like this. Odd because I didn't know the gray dog or this place existed.

These houses are a cooperatively run summer colony, once summer rentals for Jewish people from Brooklyn back in the Twenties. At times, in the months I've been here, I've seen as many people as on a suburban block walk along the soft, pine-needled paths to the laundry room or the community hall or the solid, old-fashioned swimming pool, carrying a baby or helping a child on a little pink bike or leading a file of long-legged youngsters in shorts and polka-dot sunglasses. There's life here. But beyond the boundary a sad and dreamlike landscape begins. The woods are full of derelict houses, their turrets and balconies falling, laden with moss, onto verandahs that are rotting back into tall weeds. This whole area, which was once dotted with holiday resorts for New Yorkers, has lost its role. There's an abandoned building behind the parking lot that was once the entertainment center of a neighboring colony. If you push through the long grass, past lilac bushes, to where the door yawns open, you'll see a piano inside, and scattered on the floor old records in brown-paper sleeves. "Mammy O' Mine," a medley Fox-trot played by Yerkes Jazarimba Orchestra, "Fun Mizrach Zeit" with the Merlin Sisters, and "Getzel at a Football Game." They had parties here, too.

There are cups and saucers piled under the window where tendrils of convolvulus have begun to intrude. There must have been plays up on the stage—a rusted spotlight is still trained on it. Last night at sunset Mimmo and I pushed through the long grass and startled three fawns who leaped in perfect arabesques into the woods behind. Energy came back into the old dog's floppy body for a few minutes and he was as taut as a hunter, but then he lay on the step and rested his gray head on his paws. I stood on the little dance floor inside, and listened to the gathering nightsong of the crickets and the frogs.

How exactly I got from where I was to this place is a story full of details particular to me. But the plot might have happened to anyone in middle age. The plot is about the sorrow of believing that it is too late for anything good to happen, and the joy, therefore, when something good does. It takes off from what I thought was the most commonplace relationship of all, one I gave hardly any value to compared to love: friendship. It begins when life came back into the dusty, silent house, and into my and Molly's life, through things friends did.

THAT AUTUMN, in the grim old farmhouse, an acquaintance called Luke phoned me on some practical matter and happened to find me crying. Instead of backing off apologetically, he intervened. He was a hundred miles away, where he was organizing the restoration of a great Palladian Irish house and its gardens, but though he didn't know me well, he went to the trouble of tracking Nell down and getting her to contact me—because of course it was she I was crying about—and a few hours later he rang me again to see whether I was feeling better. I put in the detail because the thing I began to learn from him that day is that friendship is something you do. He, at any rate, takes trouble for his friends. He began to watch over me a bit by phone, and eventually he invited me to be one of a house party in the mansion, and although I felt that I could hardly remember how to be with people, I went. By the following year, when I had begun to come out of my shocked state, he was sharing the house in Dublin and he began, tactfully, to clean it and put nice things in it and cook good meals.

He wasn't a bit like me—a gay man, much younger, competent across an enormous range of things and extremely sociable. I found it very hard to get used to sharing space with him. I didn't want even someone I liked intruding on my silence. He didn't ever come into my room, where I read and drank wine in the evenings, but I was always waiting to hear the click of the front door that said he had gone out, and I wasn't able to hide that from him. But he was patient. The thing I came to see was that his love of the dog and her candid love for him gave us a way to communicate. When

we were billing and cooing over Molly—which we both did
without the slightest shame—we were indicating that things
would be all right between us, that affection was warmly
there, even if it could not find direct expression. I gradually
felt myself almost physically moving back toward the world
through Luke's involvement in it, even though I still didn't
go to other people's houses or invite people into mine—the
same as my mother, who turned her back on ordinary social
pleasures once life had made her a bored and overworked
mother and housewife instead of Isolde to my father's Tristan. And as for that—passion—I was so estranged from it
that I could hardly remember what appetite was like or
what the confidence was like that would let it show. I'd forgotten how to handle all the sexual and emotional signaling
of social life, and I knew the codes were different anyhow
if you were a middle-aged woman, not to mention that spe-
cially unloved thing in a misogynistic society, a middle-aged
woman with opinions. Luke's companionship was something of a liberation from all that, and from the interests
and emphases of heterosexual couples raising children,
which shape most of Irish society. I could talk to him lightly,
glancingly. With other people, I often felt I was in a trap
made out of being shy, being sensitive to the other to the
point where I felt what they were feeling, and at the same
time and perhaps because of that empathy, being terribly
impatient to get away.

Friendship doesn't just happen once and for all, and my acceptance of a stranger in my environment came and went. But Luke didn't stop offering his companionship—he stuck with me. You'd think I'd have known that that might happen, but I did not. I fully expected to find myself alone again at any moment. Instead, I learned from him—how to hang up clothes on a washline and which of the Vermeers in the Mauritshuis exhibition were the great ones and how to cook perfect rice. And that there had been great holes in my ordinary knowledge of the world. Some very simple things have been late discoveries, which is a reward, in a way, for having lived wrong. A lot of people who were better at managing life begin to find it dull at the age I am now. Not me.

I HADN'T KNOWN, for instance, how much friends would do for each other. Around the time that Luke moved in to the house, I brought Molly to the newsroom of *The Irish Times* to show her off to a colleague who loves dogs. Sean noticed that I was still very depressed, and he invited me to come walking with him and his friends in the hills above Dublin. Well—he invited Molly, he said, but I could come too. So I dusted off my boots and made some egg and onion sandwiches and went. They were a trio of long-time male friends, and it was a big concession to let me in. But they did, and from then on, going walking with those men on a Saturday was a gift to me that I can never adequately repay, just as I can never repay Luke for restoring life to the house. There isn't an equivalent I could return. I don't know how you can show appreciation for a relief so exactly suited to an oppression.

I hadn't known that there were Gardens of Eden up there an hour from the street where I lived, where streams come sparkling and foaming down onto the floors of wide valleys, gouging their way through the bog on beds of cleanest pebbles and granite sand. In the valleys there are lichen-covered plantings of pine and spruce, and above them, heather high as a person begins, and then gorse-strewn hillsides of cropped turf slope up to where on the long ridges the surface is broken by outcrops of stone and pools of bog-water black as tar. Up there, facts are simple: wind, rain, sleet blown horizontally into faces clenched under waterproof hoods, boots sliding in mud or slipping on wet stone. On sunny days, the expanses of sweet grass were bathed in balmy air decorated by the lacy song of larks, and when we threw our backpacks down and lay beside them, the small, glossy leaves of the juniper scrub were warm to the touch. I couldn't keep up at all, the first day. It was hot, for Ireland, when we walked down a grassy lane between slender ash saplings growing out of stone walls. We came out onto a sward and crossed to the base of the next hill, where huge granite boulders spilled down the slope. We were to climb up between them through myrtle bushes and prickling gorse.

I glance down on myself now, as I write in the little wooden room in the summer colony where the boughs of the pine trees are close enough to touch the screens. I've put on a lot of weight since I stopped smoking, and isolated up here in rural New York I've been eating a lot of homemade blueberry and cherry pies, and ice cream from the gas station I can reach by bicycle. I'm five years older, too. I couldn't possibly get up that slope now. But I don't need to as long as I can still remember, as I always will, the rock against the palms of my hands, finely ground as glass, and my clumsy body trying to pull me back down as I labored upward, and the ache in my thighs from trying to pull each heavy leg up, and the triumph when we reached the grassy plateau and flopped down to drink orange squash that tasted like heaven, the valley below us swept by sun and cloud-shadow. One of the men would point out one thing, one of them another: the subtle movement in the dun and brown of the hillside across the valley that became the antique silhouette of deer on a ridge; a kestrel, plummeting down the sky; plover, rising with whirring wings from long grass; a hare, dodging up a gully.

Walking in the hills with those men became a rare but certain happiness, one of the very best things in all my life. It wasn't the outdoors that suited me perfectly—it was the outdoors together with the kind of companionship I had with those men—frank, and personal, but not for a moment intimate. The dog was ecstatic as she never was at any other time. We'd come down from the hills in the late afternoon to part in some car park, sunburned and thirsty, or in winter so frozen and wet and muddy that I could barely limp across to my own car. The best part of the day was still to come, making myself comfortable in my own house—grateful that Luke was out, and with no one else to bother about—for an evening that would be short, and certain to be followed by sleep.

See—I didn't notice that I was yet again imitating my mother. I didn't perceive that though I seemed so well, out in the open, doing healthy things with good companions, compared to my mother who spent half her life in a bar, I was securing for myself exactly the same pleasures as hers. Undisturbed reading, and drinking, and sleep, which she got from pills. If I had had children I, too, would have prevented them from making any claims on me during those evenings. If I had had a husband I, too, would have left him to see to himself while I, pink and cozy in my dressing gown after a hot bath, put a match to the fire I'd left ready, and took my chilled bottle from the fridge and served the dog and myself the food I'd prepared before I went out. A lonely life pays off in such connoisseurship. And because it is lonely you think you deserve it—you never really confront the fact that solitary pleasures erode your ties to the human race.

I think the effect of all the evenings I spent on my own like that, before and after the breakup with Nell, were what made me an autobiographer. I know that on about the third glass of wine, most nights, I would suddenly have a desire to pick up the telephone and call someone—anyone—though I never did. I just waited for the impulse to pass. All the rest of the time, I would have said, I didn't miss talking at all. But I wonder whether I was using alcohol to suppress a need to communicate. Questions about myself were accumulating within me. "How have I ended up with nobody?" was constantly drifting through my head, and I suppose I talked to an imaginary audience, trying out different explanations.

Whatever the reason, when a small publishing house in Dublin asked to bring out a selection of the opinion columns I'd been writing for *The Irish Times* and I realized that this selection would be, in the end, the only evidence that I had ever existed, I offered to write an introduction. At first I thought the introduction would be as impersonal as a column itself. But when I seriously asked myself how one introduces opinions, and what are opinions, anyway, and where do opinions come from, I realized that they came from nothing else but the experience of living a life. So, instead of writing the introduction-sized introduction the

publishers expected, in my usual genial, evasive tone, I began
to consider the possibility of making a quick sketch of the
kind of life I'd had. After all, I'd have a receptive audience
in readers so committed that they'd buy a book of old opinion columns just because they were by me. No one else
would even notice. And what had I to lose, anyway? Nothing that I could think of. I suddenly imagined myself giving
a report on middle age, though I hadn't been asked for one.

By virtue of the column, I was a pundit often called on
by the broadcasting media, and so I must have seemed to
strangers an enviably assured member of an elite. But in
daily life, though I had the company of the dog and the cat
and whatever there might be of Luke, I talked very little. It
was as if I had been led into a silent zone by a series of
choices I hadn't noticed myself making. The act of using
the introduction to write about my life as if it were over fit-
ted exactly how I felt. The good times were indeed, as far as
I was concerned, effectively over. So, now was the time to
walk around my experience and examine it, to see how it
had arrived at such emptiness. I was also attracted by the
fact that to slip an autobiographical introduction out with
the columns would be a small act of defiance. No one had
asked me, the aging woman, to write about me. It was being
an honorary man, as a commentator on public affairs, that
had brought a publisher to me. It was only because of the

public affairs that I had an opportunity now to speak about private ones. If I had been a teacher or a television producer—both things I had in fact been, never mind what most Irish women are, homemakers and mothers—I would never have been offered an opening to write about myself. But now, because of my male job, my chance had come.

There was a steamer trunk on a top shelf upstairs that I'd kept through every house move, though the key had been lost thirty years before. I went up to it now and knocked it off its shelf so that it would split open. I sat on the floor in the aroma of musty paper and read the letters in the trunk as urgently as if there were clues to treasure in them. There were letters there from people I'd been un-forgettably loved by, as well as letters, just as passionate, from people I didn't remember at all. There were letters from me to my first love. I turned over yellowing photos of my smiling young face. What, oh what, had happened to that sanguine girl?

If there had been no steamer trunk, or if there had been different things in it, what I was to put forward as my story might have been different. I think an autobiography is like any other narrative—never better than partial and provi-sional. But as well as I possibly could, and from the heart, when I managed to start my tale I told the truth. Why wouldn't I? Not very many people would ever see it.

. . .

As EVENTS in the universe go, a female Irish journalist aged fifty-six sitting down at her kitchen table to write her life story isn't very big. But I'm here in America now because of it, the lights from this apartment leaving golden lozenges on the trunks of the trees in the hot night. John, whose dog Mimmo is, and who owns this apartment, is on his way here from the city. Tonight, I'll step carefully around Mimmo, who'll sigh in his sleep, and I'll climb into bed in a room scented by the pines that cover this hillside above the still lake. I made the remark once that I could easily imagine Native American people skimming across the water in their light canoes, but John smiled at me and said that it was only a little lake, and they'd have walked around it. So when the idea came into my head that I got here all the way from Ireland in the canoe of my life story, I didn't say it. It was a bit too fanciful to say out loud. But the memoir did have magic effects and it was a vehicle. I journeyed in it from the world I saw when I looked around after breaking up with Nell, to the world I am looking at now.

BUT ONE THING journeyed with me. No matter what change came my way, I still didn't much want to be with people. Even my friends—if they hadn't kept in touch, I would have let them go. I would have drifted into friend-lessness just like my mother, who brought whatever book she was reading to the pub and sat alone and read while she drank, rather than be with people. I, too, would almost always choose to be alone. I knew loneliness like the back of my hand. And I half knew that if it was a condition I would willingly search out, it was because of her—that it seemed there was nothing I could do to lessen the power of her example or to escape from my identification with the coldness or blankness within her that made her inconsolable. I more or less accepted that she—the she-within-me—had lain in waiting for almost fifteen years to pull apart my life with Nell as if it had been a charade, and return me to loyal lone-liness. My reward made solitude even more attractive. This was the transformation I knew when present experience timeshifted into the past and revealed that there had been another layer of experience beneath the apparent one. Memory yielded up places and situations and thoughts and feelings I had known in so complex and nuanced a way that I didn't feel the need of people. The inside of my head was richly furnished without them.

But I did know that I also paid a heavy price for being alone. The failure to sustain a loving relationship with Nell came at a very late stage in the game. And I had spent the last seven Christmas holiday seasons, the ones since she left, alone, by choice, even though after the first couple of days

I got painfully depressed and bewildered. Once, in one of the early years, I tried to get involved with the Christmas holiday in a positive way. I still hadn't much money then, but I went on a cheap trip to a ski resort in Bulgaria, though I can't ski—I've never even roller-skated. I was single among the couples—so alienated from them, in fact, that they seemed faintly grotesque to me, going around in pairs leaning on each other instead of standing on their own two feet. On the mountain, as if I were trapped in a moral tale where all the evidence is rigged to teach a lesson, there was no snow, not a flake. The only thing on the slopes was a layer of exposed litter. The young Irish, stranded with nothing to do, did not behave well. At festive meals they threw bread and sprayed Bulgarian champagne all over the dining room while the waiters—old men in threadbare, much-mended white jackets—stood against the walls, looking straight ahead as if not to allow themselves to see this wantonness. Alone, I walked and walked the narrow roads between black forests.

And I remember, on the night of the millennium, when the twentieth century rolled into the twenty-first, I was in the cottage in County Clare, and the dog and I walked down the lane in the cool dark to the shore where seabirds bobbed, sleeping, on the calm night waves. I'd intended to sit on a rock and watch the fireworks display above the village across the bay—Rivebelle, as I call it to myself, after the village across the bay at whose lights Proust's sickly narrator looks in longing. But the crack and whine of the fireworks frightened Molly and she pressed against my leg, shivering, so we turned back up the lane to home and went to bed early. I did feel the presence of time, coming up to midnight, much more than on other New Year's Eves. But I was used to asking myself why I hadn't wanted to go to any of the parties I'd have been welcome at, and I knew that I didn't know the answer. I knew I could have been almost anywhere I chose; the radio was reporting great festivities from all over the world and I had acquaintances everywhere and the money to travel. I also knew that there was no point in asking myself why I wasn't in any of those glamorous places; the answer was that I didn't know.

We went to bed long before twelve o'clock, the dog and I. She could still hear the howitzer noise of fireworks, and she padded into the bedroom and jumped up to press herself into the curve of my back. The phone did ring a few times but I didn't get up and go in to the other room to answer it. I thought, "There'll be time enough in the morning to find out who's thinking of me." But in the morning I discovered that I'd forgotten to switch on the answering machine.

Looking back on it now, I see that piece of forgetfulness as extraordinarily expressive. I must have known that I wasn't in any real, objective sense alone. There were people out there who loved me or might love me or in any case had me in their thoughts. But I was set on not letting love in. Or—on not cooperating with the actions of love. If my heart was to be reached, then it would have to be in some way that I hadn't lifted a finger to invite. And I ask myself, still not knowing the answer, what shrine was I worshipping at, lying there in the dark, stiff with loneliness, listening to the phone ring in the next room and not going in to answer it?

MY REPORT, then, from middle age, has a tension to it, because it swings between the two poles of wanting to be alone and being lonely. Middle age is the least talked about of all the seasons of life, and yet it seems to me the most exacting. It is adolescence come again at the other side of adulthood—the matching bookend—in its uneasiness of identity, its physical surprises and the strength it takes to handle it. A person who feels herself still uncertain, still tentative, still a learner, is startled to see beginning in her age group, a winnowing-out, a next-to-Last-Judgment. I look now past bland young faces to the ones with grooves down the upper lips and indistinct jaw lines and wrinkles around the eye sockets. I'm looking to see whether my contemporaries know how to do this growing older stuff better than I do. How's their health? What people do they have in their lives? Do they look serene? Do they look happy? Do I look as happy as they?

I listed my circumstances after Nell moved out—that it seemed to me that I had no one to love or to love me, that I had no child, not much money, that I drank too much, that my family was not part of my life, that I had no plans. Every single one of those circumstances has changed. I have had so many good things happen to me in the last six of my middle years that I feel now like a pioneer who has crossed a continent and reached the top of a final hill and has just caught sight of fertile fields below. Even if they are fields already colored by autumn. But I'm uneasy underneath. I am not used to being given things for no reason. If my present good fortune is a reward, when did I earn it? Or can it be that life rewards you not for what you do but for what you are? If so, all I can say is I threw away twenty years, if you add up the wasted ones, relying on reading and drink and sleeping tablets and fugitive emotions. I wasn't half the person I could have been, and even the people who cared about me had no respect for me. I have won a few skirmishes against self-defeat lately. But I haven't got much confidence. I do not know whether I will be able to come down from the ridge and into the beautiful autumn fields.

I used to know a couple who fought and feuded their way through the middle years, though anyone could see that they really loved each other. "Stick it out!" I used to say to her every time she threatened to leave him. "In the end you'll come out onto Golden Pond!" And they did; and that's what I want for myself, too. To be finished with turbulence. I didn't know that I was embarking on a journey when I wrote the first words of *Are You Somebody?*, and I didn't believe that calm water might be waiting for me, too. But I see now that a movement began then that won't be completed until I glide into stillness. Maybe because I can glimpse the lake from the room where I write this, I sometimes think that I'm getting there, that I'm almost there.

CHAPTER TWO

Germination

IN THE CENTER OF DUBLIN, JUST UP
from the neon and burger joints of the wide main street,
there are terraces and squares of tall Georgian houses that
have become homely over the centuries and are warrens
now of different uses. One of these is the Irish Writers'
Center. Before I could get my autobiographical introduction started, I had to sit on a plastic chair under the elegant
stucco ceiling of what, in the eighteenth century, would have
been a reception room, gazing morosely at the teacher's
wonderful shoes on her shapely legs, a reluctant enrollee in
a six-session writing course. My fellow students looked at
me a bit closely the first day because they knew who I was—
as far as they were concerned I was a writer already. But I'd
gone blank when I tried to write the introduction I'd prom-
ised. I couldn't take possession of the first-person voice. I

couldn't manage an "I" if it was going to be real, as opposed to the "I" in my opinion columns which was cheerfully fake-authoritative. I had all kinds of theories why this was so—for example, that it was because I was Irish and female and had had the message drummed into me all my life that female isn't nearly as interesting and important as male. Now if I were an American, I thought, with a sturdy tradition of civil rights behind me, I'd say "I" proudly. But theories weren't helping me. It had got to the point where I was afraid to answer the phone in case it was the publisher inquiring about the introduction. So, in desperation, I signed up for the writing course. I remember how the windscreen wipers pushed the streaming rain from side to side of black, gleaming streets as I drove into the city the nights of the classes, and how much I resented leaving my fire and my glass of wine and how much I didn't want to meet other people and didn't want to make an effort. But I had to.

It had been Christmas week when Tony Glavin, an American writer living in Dublin and working as an editor with a small Irish publishing house, met me to suggest making a book of my newspaper columns. He'd heard me speak a few years earlier at the University of Massachusetts at Amherst, in a lecture series about Ireland, and had taken an interest in my journalism since then. The streets I walked down to meet him were washed with rain, and there were smears of red and gold and traceries of silver reflected from decorated shop windows and thin carols coming from speakers over doorways, and Tony was standing outside the café because of the press of bustling Christmas shoppers inside. I felt my outsider status at the holiday festival very keenly. Everyone else seemed to be pressed for time, but all I had to do was put the dog and the cat and some food in the car and head for County Clare, where there was nothing waiting for me. It must have been because I wanted to assert something about the me that had the opinions—the whole me, the me who was a person with nothing to do at Christmas—that I turned to Tony and said, "I'll write an introduction to the columns, if you like." I had no clear idea what kind of introduction I meant, but something to do with being on my own at Christmas made me want to leave my mark.

From the first instant, I had to fight with inner voices that mocked my self-importance. "You aren't helping me to get through life!" I shouted back at them. "No one is helping me to get through life! So what do I owe anyone? I owe nobody anything!" But as my intention became clearer to me, I got more afraid of what people would say about my egotism in reprinting old opinion columns in the first place, and compounding the offense by adding a personal introduction. I'm as sensitive as the next person to the local pecking order, and I knew that if anyone in Dublin could get away with thinking as highly of themselves as I seemed to be doing, that someone wasn't me. One half of me agreed with the begrudgers. "Who does she think she is?" I'd find myself thinking—about myself. But the other half said, "The hell with them."

The contradictions within me kept my tongue tied. That was what sent me on the writing course, where, it turned out, some of the others were so talented that I looked forward all week to hearing them read out the assignments the teacher gave us, which I myself was not able to do. I was driving home from the class one cold night, laughing to myself because the homework the teacher had set us was to write a thousand words about something that happened in a bathroom. "Not sex!" she'd said, wagging her finger at the men in our group because they had an amazing ability to find a sex angle to every subject, no matter how apparently unpromising. I was wondering what the guys were going to do this time, when abruptly my laughter cut off. I'd remembered that my mother died on the floor of the bathroom in the small, rented apartment that saw the end of all that she was.

The laughter must have opened a door within me. "Of course lots of people must die in bathrooms," I gabbled to myself. "They're the only room in the house that you can lock, usually, bathrooms. Well, for poor people. Poor people must die in bathrooms—" But the film I tried never to watch had begun. I saw my mother's death. I hurried to the kitchen table and with my coat still on I held my hands over the keyboard, imagining how it must have been. She didn't lock the door, the last time she was ever to touch it. She was alone in that horrible little flat. I had always avoided that bathroom, because of the glimpses of private things I did not want to know about my parents—indigestion tablets, yellow marks on the porcelain of the toilet bowl. Now I saw her stumbling as the dizziness started, I saw her beginning to fall, I saw her slumping halfway down, then all the way down, a thump, then stillness, silence, the person she had been become an ungainly shape, her poor face pressed against the shabby floor. The only good thing is that she wouldn't have been frightened. Drunks are more than used to dizziness, and as it was, her face was marked from recent falls.

That was the beginning of my writing, though I soon went back in time to my childhood and started over again there—not that that kept my mother out of the narrative. I don't know the right name for what I wrote. It wasn't an autobiography—that's a much larger enterprise than I attempted and it needs a big, solid view of your own importance to sustain it. Yet it wasn't merely an autobiographical essay—I did hope by the end to have put in enough raw material to be known, not so much by the reader as by myself. What I was writing went this way and that way. It had no real theme. It was more a cry of protest than anything else, and detail accumulated as I tried to explore why my life seemed to have come to nothing in spite of great promise and many good and happy times and people. The best word for what I made of the introduction is probably "memoir," which is the slightest of the forms of reminiscence, though it's a word that has too much of the aesthete about it, too much of the something perfectly formed. It is a word that suggests that the author's shaping of the memories is the point; not the memories. It is too smooth for the random, ragged way my past came back to me that summer as I sat at my laptop, half watching Molly watch the moths that stumbled in through the open window on the warm air, half lost in the past.

THERE IS AN IDEA current in the prevailing culture that writing about something that pains you heals the pain. I was not, when I began writing my life story, and am not now, healed of my mother. But you do gain a small distance from anything by keeping it in suspension in your mind while you work at finding the words to fit it. The process is so slow and incremental that you don't notice its effect, but the point is that it is a process. I found out when I was a little girl that if you're crying uncontrollably and want to stop, the thing is to do something useful with your tears—water a plant, say. They'll dry up of themselves. The same happens when you try to make sentences out of painful material: the material lightens as it is put to work.

This relief to the individual is justification enough for self-revelation in some cultures. But not in Ireland. In Ireland there are sanctions for speaking out—on the lowest level by sour murmurs behind your back that you're in it for the money, and on a much more serious level by reproach for breaking the consensus that previous generations kept intact. *How could you do it to your poor mother?* they say. *Couldn't you have left the poor woman her good name? What right have other people to know what went on behind closed doors in your family?* The lid was kept on in Ireland, no matter what. Everyone might know that he beats her or she pilfers from shops or they've been up to Dublin for cancer tests, but as long as nothing is spoken, all concerned can hold their heads up and chat away with the neighbors, standing around after Mass on a Sunday. Silence was the defensive strategy of a people who did not believe situations can be changed and did not imagine they could ever get away from each other. And it made a kind of sense—at least everyone concerned kept a shred of dignity. My father took this line about my mother's alcoholism; it wasn't there if it wasn't spoken about. This did in fact keep open the possibility of her behaving well, and in the last years of his life he took her on a few holidays abroad, and she, freed from any hint of being a mother, for once not bored, and having him all to herself, loved every moment of those escapes.

I wasn't an expert in denial like he was. Nor, of course, did I understand the context in which he saw her, or have access to his memories of her as a young woman and his lifelong private knowledge of her. I wanted to talk straight out about the harm she did, once he and romance betrayed her, and about how he had not prevented the harm. I didn't need permission from the family to do that—none of us ever do ask the others for permission for anything. Nevertheless, even an apparently flexible family is a family, and I needed to introduce my project in some better way than just sending my brothers and sisters copies of the finished book. So at draft stage I visited the three older women— girls, as I always think of them, and as they're always called—approaching each in a different tone, just as they use different tones with me. Their network of liaisons and influence elsewhere in the larger family group made them representatives of the whole nine, when I set off like a knight of old on his trusty steed to visit their territories.

My sister Grainne's bailiwick is in an estate of ranch-style houses, with picture windows onto communal front lawns and leafy streets. The whole place speaks of safety, security, cleanliness. We were sitting in her kitchen with the patio door open to the garden when Hodge, a blackly glistening apparition, came slinking through the roses to see what was going on. "He likes living in a suburb," she said. It had never occurred to me that a cat might have lifestyle preferences, but it may have been true that the way I lived struck him as unacceptably bohemian. He fell in love with Grainne's partner, anyway, when I left him with them for a few days; I came back to find a routine of Hodge watching television sitting peacefully on Derry's lap, and then going upstairs with Derry and sleeping on Derry's chest, nose peeping from the duvet. He had chosen to leave me. We spoke about the cat and little else, because I hadn't given Grainne any of my draft to read, this visit being understood to be not really personal but more a respectful call on the head of state, which is what Grainne is, as the eldest in the family. She made me a little meal with a wonderful economy of gesture. No one could more precisely possess a space than she does in her kitchen, yet our mother was always as clumsy as a stranger in hers. Not wanting to be like your mother must be a very powerful motive.

Then I clip-clopped off to Deirdre's castle, which is a modest terrace house usually crammed with people and activity. Deirdre is the next one down after me. She and her husband are an old-style, devoted, married couple, very happy Catholics, whose largely joyful task, since they joined up as teenagers, has been looking after their seven children and any friends, in-laws, grandchildren, distant cousins,

neighbors, et cetera, who happen to pass by. I dismounted
from my steed long enough for a mug of tea and rhubarb
tart, and Deirdre tamped tobacco into the little pipe she
smokes and got ready to relish a conversation about what
she really likes talking about, which is classic English liter-
ature. She helps local children study the novels and poems
that are set for school examinations, and although or because she left formal education herself at sixteen, she absolutely loves the texts. When she rang me a few days later
to say that she'd read the pages of *Are You Somebody?* that I'd
left with her and in spite of personal reservations—which is
a gentle way of saying that she does not share my values at
all—I had her blessing, it meant a great deal to me. I would
have gone on, even in the face of her disapproval. But it was
the first fruit of the whole enterprise that she chose, as always, to think the best of me, and that I got the benefit of
her respect for writing.

Then I ventured on an embassy overseas, if you call
going to London that, to Noreen's place, which really is like
a castle—a top floor maisonette in London with a balcony
and a turret and many sloping roofs among thick chestnut
trees. Noreen's the next sister down after Deirdre. She took
the printout I'd brought into her room and stayed in there,
reading, for hours.

"You're not intending to publish this by any chance, are
you?" was her opening remark delivered in a tone of icy in-

credulity when she finished. I got such a shock that tears came to my eyes. "Don't you realize what you've done here?" she said when she saw my face. "Don't you see that you're trying to get your own back at anyone who's ever hurt you in your life?"

"I am?" I said, astonished. "Where? I don't see anything like that!"

"There! And there! And there!"

She stood behind me while I went through the whole thing on the laptop, deleting this bit here and that bit there. I don't even remember what the bits were, the same as mothers, they tell me, don't remember the pain of child-birth.

"Now it has an unnatural air of saintly understanding," I grumbled, but I was very, very glad that Noreen had shown me what I couldn't see for myself.

I stayed on with her and her partner and worked on the draft for a final week. I didn't ask her to look at it again— once was quite enough to exhaust her patience—but I was conscious of her intelligence and her goodwill very near. I liked those days very much, working at the big table in a bay window until she and her partner came home every evening. It took a lot of the loneliness out of writing. The flat floats above trees in old back gardens. Outside my window there was a poplar and in it a pigeon sitting on a nest, and I used to watch bird and nest sway in the dappled green of the sunlit branches. Years later, when I was trying to think of a setting for a happy time for the novel I wrote, I used an attic flat in London and a nest like the one in the tree outside, and I'm sure now that that was because working on *Are You Somebody?* in a setting where there were other people who wished me well was so unexpectedly comforting.

MEMOIR IS, surely, a genre that leaves a lot of blood on the tracks. Unless it is nearly completely solipsistic, it involves reporting on other people who have real lives. And the autobiographer knows in advance that there is going to be an afterlife, when the people within the book read it. It is therefore, of all seemingly candid forms, the one most likely to be shaped by diplomatic necessities. If I were the biographer of an autobiographer, I'd be very interested to discover what they felt they had to clear out of the way before telling their story.

For myself, once I came back from my trip around the sisters, I could finish off my book. One day I saw what I would call it. I had presented a books program on television a few years before, and for a while I was very well known, but it was a minority interest program, of course, and thousands of people must have seen my face just long enough to change channels. I know that occasionally in pubs or supermarkets a woman would be egged on by her friends to check out whether I was that person they'd glimpsed on the screen. The daring one would come up to me. "Are you somebody?" she'd say. The phrase came into my head one day, and took on resonance. How do people come to believe they are of value? Could a person looking back on their life gather from it the self-approval to reply to that question, "Yes, I am!"

My final act was to choose the columns that this memoir would be the introduction to, trying to pick ones that weren't too dated. Then I sent the designer an image I loved for the cover. It is a drawing by the Irish artist Alice Maher of a little girl. She has feathery angel's wings but her sturdy little legs end in red rubber boots. She has her hands on her hips and interrogates the spectator, mysterious and fierce.

How could I have thought that that was the end of that?

A couple of years later, on a rainy night in Hollywood, I was walking up Sunset Boulevard to the Chateau Marmont for a showdown with a man I mentioned in the memoir. I hadn't reckoned on any fallout outside the family because I thought only a handful of people would ever see the book. But I would have done well to remind myself that one party to a shared experience only knows one side of it. I was shaking in my shoes in Los Angeles because I'd described an episode in Dublin, when I was a girl, when an American student I was flirting around with in his flat answered the doorbell and came back and ". . . forced himself into me. After a few awful minutes of red-hot pain he collapsed onto my shocked body, sobbing dreadfully. He sat on the edge of the bed after a while and put his head in his hands. 'That was a telegram,' he said. 'My mother is dead.'" I described the episode as I remembered it. I had almost forgotten that this man was, of course, a real person—I hadn't heard him mentioned for maybe thirty years. So I was truly horrified when one day I opened my e-mail to find that the book had somehow come his way in California, and he had discovered my e-address, and there was something he wanted me to know. According to him it hadn't happened that way at all. And he sent me a passage, from an unpublished novel of his, written long ago, which gave his account of the same event.

> *Somehow she got it into her head that what he really needed was something to get lost in, something that would make him forget what she called the "terrible news." To her this meant sex. He didn't feel like making love at the moment, he just wanted to sit down and think, to realize the death, but she was determined to make him forget and he didn't know how to stop her. They were*

alone in the basement flat, they went into his small, untidy room,
they undressed and they made love.

And much more. I suppose it's something, I said to myself as I read, that neither of us quite forgot the occasion.

He was looking out the window of the lounge at the rain
sluicing down into the empty swimming pool when the
Chateau Marmont bellboy pointed him out. I took a deep
breath and arranged my face. You need a bit of courage
when someone who last saw you when you were a girl is
going to turn around, as soon as you say his name, and see a
woman who's coming up to sixty. There was also the matter
of the disputed near-rape. "How come other writers don't
get into this sort of trouble?" I asked myself, but as it turned
out, there was no trouble at all. We had two large drinks
very fast and made cheerful small talk. We never spoke
about the night his mother died. Or, at least, I looked down
at the floor and mumbled something about how amazing it
was, the way different people could remember things differently, and then we slid off onto some other subject.

THAT MAN and I hadn't ever mattered to each other. But
the same was not true of the former lover I called Rob,
whom the memoir also brought into conflict with my version of events, which I had decided was reality. I met Rob

when I was doing a postgraduate degree at Oxford and fell in love with him with all the commitment and hope of that time of life, and I never completely recovered from the stormy ten years when he was the center of my life. He had a huge influence on me, both for good, in all I picked up from his marvelous mind, and for bad, in the ways we failed each other. By the time I wrote *Are You Somebody?* we had been on distant, amiable terms for decades and I had no designs on the real, happily married Rob and no regrets either about my own long and richly rewarding relationship with Nell. But there were parts of London so imprinted with the intensity of what I had felt for him when I was young, that when I was in them I was always waiting for him to come around the corner. In those places, I'd be apprehensive all day, and, finally, disappointed, and this sequence had a life of its own—there was nothing to stop me picking up the phone if I genuinely wanted to see him. In Dublin, there's an eighteenth-century square where I had had a flat up under the rooftops. I went any other way, so as not to pass the house on that square where he and I had been so happy, when he would come over from England on the ferry in the early morning and ring the bell and I would wake from sleep and throw the keys down and jump back under the bedclothes, my heart pounding as loud as his feet on the stairs. I couldn't entirely brush away the vestiges of all that I had felt then.

I can hardly believe, now, that I sent Rob an early draft of the memoir, including all the bits about him, and asked for his help with editing—he is a famously skilled editor. But I genuinely wasn't worried about his reaction—I thought he of all people would see that I'd put in the best things about him and left out a great deal to his and my discredit. At the same time, I was gratified that he was at last going to hear my side of things. When he had left me, at the end of the ten years, he left a note on the table saying "Back Tuesday" and he never came back and never explained. Now, as well as getting the benefit of his professional advice, he would see at last how much he had hurt me. It beggars belief that I could have thought this would be fine with him. But I did. I really did. And when, in reply, an absolutely final letter of rejection came from him, I could hardly take in the words. I stood with the page in my hand in the hallway in Dublin, bent over, as if I had been punched.

I SUPPOSE MY UNCONSCIOUS—which I look on as a mischievous alter ego living within me but going about her own errands—wanted to finally get rid of the burden of him. Who would have thought that writing a memoir could serve such a useful purpose? But Rob was a detail of history. What was really important was what *Are You Somebody?* might mean to the woman I'd lived with for many years.

We were very close, still, Nell and I, a year after we split up. It took a long, long time for all the warmth to go out of what had been between us. I had no appetite for writing about our life together; the loss was too great and the parting too recent, and I was still too obsessed with apportioning blame. So I decided to skip all the rest and to indicate how much fun we'd had at our best, and how well we'd been able to experience things when we were together, by describing some of our mildly intrepid travels. The anecdotes I told were intended to indicate the quality of the companionship we had had. I was taken aback, not to mention hurt, when she told me later that she bitterly resented this oblique approach. But then I never realized, never having written before about people I'd known intimately, that they're almost bound to be offended. Even the most flattering of sketches must always be a shock to other people's complex sense of themselves. The writer knows she is picking only a few details from the living whole of a reminiscence, whereas all the reader sees is that what is on the page is thin.

Once, long before when we were walking down a street, a poet we knew stopped the two of us and described a poetry festival in a town on what he said was a magically deep lake, with a rare and delicious fish in it, between Macedonia and Albania. When I finished *Are You Somebody?* I asked Nell if she would come to that lake with me. And we did go there, crawling up the mountains into Albania on a work-man's bus from Thessaloniki and getting entry visas at the sad border post with its broken cardboard walls and dim lightbulb. In Albania, the children were feral and the an-cient churches were gouged with graffiti, but people asked us into their homes and a man climbed a tree to shake down walnuts for us, and in the half-derelict hotel on Lake Ochrid, where water leaked from every pipe, we could hear ballroom music from the shabby *salon* where the locals were dancing. In our happier days we would have gone down-stairs and joined in. We walked out of that village along the lake on a sunny morning and through a modern, efficient border crossing into the Balkan country known to itself as Macedonia. We ate the exquisite fish in the town the poet told us about, and bought postcards. But the postcards, I noticed one day, were like an illustration of the silences that now fell between the two of us. Because Macedonia doesn't want to acknowledge that Albania is there—or at least hadn't wanted to at the time the postcards were printed— Albania was airbrushed out. I stood there with a postcard in my hand looking across the lake at the Albanian mountains. Look down at the postcard—no mountains, just air. I didn't share the thought with Nell. That's what it was like, too, writing *Are You Somebody?* without giving a major role to our years together. But it wasn't possible for me then to stabi-lize a view of our relationship. And I still cannot. I think part of this is a function of age. When you're twenty, you get over a two-year relationship in, maybe, six months. When you're thirty, it takes longer—two years, might it be, to get over a six- or seven-year relationship? Then how long will it take to absorb the loss of a nearly fifteen-year relationship that ends when the couple are in their fifties? The answer is—very long.

It turned out to have been wishful thinking to hope that our holiday selves could keep going as healthy limbs even though the body of our daily selves had been cut away. We parted, this time for good, when we came out of the neighboring countries and back down into Greece. We were at a railway station. She was going back to Ireland; I was taking a train to a small, ordinary Greek town, picked at random from the map, for no better reason than to spend some time completely alone. In an unexpected twist, I was furiously angry with her. I'd given her a draft of the whole of *Are You Somebody?* And now she revealed that she'd shown it to a woman friend of her own, to see what this woman thought of it. She didn't trust her own judgment about literary things, Nell said—she wanted this woman to tell her whether the memoir was good or bad. She also wanted this woman to pronounce on whether or not I'd been fair to Nell in the memoir. I stood on the platform hissing things like, "Who said you could show it to her? That's my private business! Who gave you permission to show my private stuff to a stranger? Who said you could do that? How dare you! That's *private*."

I asked myself afterward, in the solid little Greek town as I sat under a hanging television set at a plastic-covered table in a café full of old men, how I could possibly justify this reaction about something I myself intended to publish. There were obvious-enough reasons for some of my anger, no doubt. But why couldn't I bear my scrutiny being turned back on me? I gave myself permission to talk about people, but look how I felt at the thought of those two talking about me! I wanted to control the characters and actions of everyone in my story. I didn't want anything from any reader but acquiescence. It was as if I wanted them all completely passive, or as if a memoir is not at all what memoir writers think it is, but an arranging of material that, if left lying around, would explode and leave blood and guts all over the place.

Novels are complete when they are finished, but the memoir changes its own conclusion by virtue of being written. The words it chooses to describe relationships are another development in those relationships. The hostility I provoked in others and in myself seems to me now part of a breakout from imprisoning myths, such as the myth of still loving someone who is not there to be loved anymore. I hadn't realized before I wrote *Are You Somebody?* that I for one need constantly to relearn a simple thing—that I do

not understand other people as they understand themselves. Rob's reaction, and much more importantly, Nell's,
made me understand that I am one person and other people are themselves, and not what I have decided they are. I
see the beginning of some kind of learning about how to be
a member of the social world in these realizations connected with writing a memoir. And that sliver of clarity was
part of a wider clarifying of the muddle in my head. I don't
know whether it is the same for everyone middle-aged or
just for people who drank as much as I, but I really did not
remember, before I sat down that summer, exactly what
happened when. Whatever can be said about the other al-
leged therapeutic effects of autobiographical writing, that
one works—tidying your memory the way you'd tidy a clut-
tered room. I was not at all the same person, when I handed
the manuscript over to the publisher, as I'd been when I
began. A memoir may always be retrospective, but the past
is not where its action takes place.

I HAVE AN OLD FRIEND I don't see very often, but when
I do we have a good lunch and split a bottle of good wine.

This particular lunch was in the dining room of the
Clarence Hotel in Dublin, which I like going to because it's
owned by U2 and they don't need any money so perhaps the
profit margin isn't too outrageous. The Sancerre's good, too.

"And when's the book coming out?" my friend said when we had all the important news out of the way, such as how much weight we each hadn't managed to lose and how her son was doing at school.

I hurried to correct her. "It isn't a *book,* number one," I said. "It's only an introduction. And there's no launch or anything—you don't do that for a collection of oul' columns that have been out before. So number two, it isn't *coming out.* It'll *be* out, I think in a couple of weeks. It'll be *out,* whereas at the moment it's *in*—"

"Nuala." She cut across me. I can see her still and the way her head tilted down a little because she's taller than I, and the smile on her face when she said—gently, but definitely:

"Nuala. It is your work. *Stand by it.*"

I HAVE REPEATED that phrase on many occasions when I've been talking to audiences. Sometimes I've led up to it by telling how I'd put *Are You Somebody?* out of my mind when I'd finished it, honestly never expecting anything to come of it, and then my friend said three words to me and the three words were words that changed my whole view of what I'd done. They were words that made me want to look after what I'd written as if it were part of me, like a child. She had leaned across and said three words that couldn't be more ordinary, but they had stopped me apologizing for what I'd written and made me want to get the best life I could for it. And the three words were "Stand by it!"—and then when I've said the words, there's been a gasp of understanding. They're words of real power.

And that's what I was doing when I offered myself to go on *The Late Late Show,* which is Ireland's big television chat show, the day my book was published. I was standing by it.

EVERYONE KNOWS that the razzamatazz entry—the TV host with his arms spread wide and a big smile on his face, the band blaring out a fanfare, the studio audience applauding wildly, everyone looking expectantly at the top of the shiny steps where tonight's mystery guest is about to appear—everyone knows that that isn't for you and me. That's for Liza Minnelli and Tony Bennett, and so on. I stood in the dark behind the set shaking from head to foot while the host belted out the words:

"And will you welcome, *please*—"

The floor manager shoved me toward the opening at the top of the steps.

"—*Nuala! O! Faolaín!*"

Another shove out into the lights.

I had to walk down the shiny steps smiling madly though I could all but hear the audience's disappointed mutter as their anticipation subsided. No film stars tonight, then.

The host embraced me and sat me down opposite him and the camera crept in to take the close-up of me. He leaned forward to begin the interview.

"Well, well," he chuckled, not altogether genially, "well, Nuala, you've slept with a lot of men, haven't you?"

I HAD WAITED to go on in a small dressing room, almost paralyzed with fear, because I knew my reputation and my family's and Nell's was going to be changed by the interview, and my standing with colleagues and bosses and former lovers and the nuns who'd taught me—anyone I could think of. But there really is such a thing as grace. It's the word I want to use, anyway, for a rightness of behavior that kicks in out of nowhere.

"Let me be honest!" I implored—of myself, I suppose, though I vaguely imagined that I was asking God. "Let me pause and try to find a truthful answer, no matter what I'm asked." Somehow I understood that almost nothing in the situation was under my control—I didn't know how long the interview was going to be, for example, and I had no idea what the host had thought of the book. But I knew that my own self was under my control and so was what I could try to be out there. I won that moment of lucidity from the panic I was in and it was enough to see me through. The interview recovered from the snide opening; the host's professional genius picked up signals of sympathy for me from the very way the audience breathed, and he dropped the arch tone and became warm and serious. He'd known my father, of course, and he'd have seen my mother occasionally, attending this and that with my father, makeup on, hands shaking, face set in a forced smile. He understood the tragedy of the pair of them, who had set out in life so full of charm and intelligence, and loving each other so much. He brought up the subject of my living with Nell, too, she being a famous firebrand. The domestic side of her came as news to everyone—I imitated her exasperation, rolling out pizza dough, at the way it always happens that one corner has receded by the time the other corner is stretched into place. I hadn't meant to do that—I hadn't had answers prepared for any of his questions. But he had settled on a fond, calm tone for the interview, and in that tone it was more natural to talk about Nell as a partner in homemaking than as anything else. When he moved on to my feelings at being in my late fifties, without children and without a partner, he was like the most delicate and unjudgmental of confessors.

But the way he and I were able to talk to each other, even in public, even under arc lights, was also because of me, and the moment of grace before the show.

I consider the twenty minutes of that interview one of

the highlights of my life, because I did reach down to a rare honesty for it.

If ever I get married, that's what I hope to do before I say the vows. Look into myself and find the place where I really mean what I say.

I WAS UP in the hills above Dublin the next day, with Molly and two of the men I walked with on Saturdays. My phone was out of order at home, so they were the first people I talked to who'd seen the interview.

"You did great last night," one of them said, when we were eating our sandwiches in the shelter of an outcrop of boulders.

"I wouldn't wish it on my worst enemy," I said. "I thought I'd die of nerves."

"He didn't take it seriously at first," the other one said.

"I know! Did you notice his opening shot? About all the men I'm supposed to have slept with?"

"He got manners fast."

"The audience put manners on him. I could feel them willing him to talk to me properly."

"You were crying at the end, weren't you?" one of the men said. "Weren't those tears in your eyes? When the caller rang in to say she'd already bought the book and it was marvelous?"

"Oh, I don't know," I said. "Crying's putting it too strongly . . ."

I didn't say that I was almost overcome by that interview and the applause at the end when the host hugged me, and that I slipped away and went straight home because I thought a wave of affection had rolled down from the studio audience and I wanted to go to bed with it wrapped around me.

That day, we came down from the hills early because it was a harsh winter afternoon with the threat of snow in a low sky. I remember that I put my hands down the waistband of my trousers under my panties against the skin of my belly to try to keep them flexible. They went stiff again as I drove home, and I had to get straight into a bath where my skin turned a mottled beetroot red. I had my supper and drank my wine and went to bed, pleasantly exhausted. I didn't know that I was in the last hours of the old world. I had never stopped to think what writing a memoir that other people are avid to read would mean. Next day I heard that the bookstores were swamped with people looking for *Are You Somebody?* My life story had taken on value. Even if they didn't like what they read, they'd chosen to read it. Something, now, was made of my existence—all of it, not just the public part.

And it seemed the readers did like me. I had managed, by introducing the book on television, to reach an audience over the head of literary editors and reviewers—to bypass the so-called critical process. And the timing was perfect. Ireland, at the end of the twentieth century, was beginning to allow self-knowledge. Some of the worst, most brutal stories about life in Irish institutions had already been told, and there had been revelations from the sacred site of the family, too, that could not be managed by denial. I had nothing very sensational to say, but the way I wrote about myself was more candid than any Irish woman had yet been, outside the more oblique forms of fiction and song and poetry. My account of myself with its final note of resignation, of disappointment accepted—sincerely meant when it was written—was out of date as soon as I went on that chat show. For a while, I could hardly walk down an Irish street without being recognized and, in many cases, extravagantly thanked. My loneliness had changed. In one way it migrated deeper within me. In another, it had been purged of its darkness by becoming the property of a large public.

TONY GLAVIN and I were totally gobsmacked. For a few weeks in Ireland the book was such a sensation that bookstores sold it straight from the wholesaler's cartons—there wasn't time to put it on the shelves. The small publishing house rose to the occasion magnificently, the owner carting boxes of new print runs around in his own Jeep to deliver with his own hands. It was a purely happy story for all of us. Within six months the introduction was bought for England and Australia—the opinion columns were dropped, and from then on it was published just as a memoir. I added an afterword to the original at that stage—it had become ludicrous to present myself as someone whose disappointing life was essentially over, when my life was patently bursting with new growth. I also wanted to give a flavor of the letters that had begun to flood in, since the ardor of the response to such an unsensational memoir as *Are You Somebody?* was very important, even if it was also a mystery.

But also, I wasn't the same person I had been when I wrote *Are You Somebody?* Because a young brother of ours decided not to live. He was an alcoholic, like our mother, and he'd gradually lost everything he had ever valued, and he was in very bad physical condition. He'd ended up in a room near London Airport, and he sat down in a chair in that room with a supply of vodka and refused to eat or to see a doctor or accept help of any kind, and although it took a few months, he achieved his ambition, and he passed on. His daughter told me he turned a greenish color toward the end. It was an awful way to die. He was the first of our flesh and blood to go, and I didn't know any way of grasping what he'd done or of assigning some meaning to it, except by writing about it. I am surprised that more memoirists don't become serial memoirists, because it is a precious thing to be allowed to talk about yourself in public, not for reasons of simple exhibitionism but because the attempt to describe your experience to an audience pushes you forward into an understanding of it.

A YEAR LATER there was the most unexpected publishing development of all. America had already played a key part in this little saga, since Tony Glavin, an American, had marked me down in Amherst, in America. Now, in Dublin, he and his wife went out for a few drinks one night with friends, and they were joined by a friend of a friend who worked in schoolbook publishing in the Boston area. Tony, ever alert to opportunity, pressed a copy of *Are You Somebody?* onto Pat for her to take back to America in the remote hope that she might come across somebody who might like to publish it. Which she, amazingly, did. A friend of hers, called Michael Jacobs, had a senior executive job in publishing in New York, but he found the time to read *Are You Somebody?,* and without knowing any of us, out of sheer enthusiasm for the book itself, he persistently took it around to his contacts. And on Saint Patrick's Day in 1997, in Berlin where I'd gone on a package tour weekend, the phone in my hotel room rang. It was afternoon, and I reached for it from under the bedclothes—you can imagine how iron-cold it must have been that in a new city I was back in bed in the afternoon. Tony's voice: "Hang on to your hat, Nuala. Are you ready for a piece of news? Michael's done it! *Are You Somebody?* has been bought! It's going to be published in the States!"

Which is how I came, exactly a year later, on Saint Patrick's Day, 1998, to be sitting on the set of *Good Morning America* at something like 7:30 in the morning, drinking green soup and singing "When Irish Eyes Are Smiling."

I'd arrived in New York the day before. I couldn't sleep for nervousness, and I was awake when they called me very early in the hotel. I got up from my knees where I had been praying to nobody in particular and went to shower. It was dark still, just before a cold dawn, and way down below there was only as much traffic in the wide streets as in a sepia photograph. These are hard moments, and I often thought of my father when the challenge of making a presentation of myself had to be met. He put on a façade all the time. He did it for a living. If there's one thing I know from him, it's that if you're on duty you may not weep or wail. You may not miss a deadline. You may not say you don't feel like making an appearance. You must take a deep breath, and go out there smiling, acting naturally until you relax enough to be natural.

I was taken around the corner to the TV studio and into the makeup room, where the affable man in the chair beside me, both of us trussed up under capes like babies being fed, turned out to be Frank McCourt, at that time one of the most famous men on the planet and a hero of mine—I'd read a proof copy of *Angela's Ashes* before I or anyone else in Ireland had heard of him, and I'd recognized at once that it had Dickensian qualities and that it was destined to become the most famous book by an Irishman since *Ulysses*. I said so, too, in *The Irish Times*. But I never thought I'd meet Frank. He was so laidback that I relaxed too, and in we went to the studio as if it were the most normal thing in the world, where we were put on a sofa between monitors taking feeds from the preparations for Paddy's Day parades all over the States, with black policemen in green wigs, half-frozen majorettes in little green skirts twirling batons, folk groups, banner wavers, pipe bands, hordes of Riverdance clones, green beer and cheerleaders with green pom-poms. *Are You Somebody?* was discussed for maybe a minute and a half maximum, though in the hands of these practiced entertainment interviewers, that gets quite a lot said. Then there was a song, I think. Then there was an excursion into politics as sudden as it was brief. The male interviewer leaned toward Frank and said earnestly, "Could you explain one thing to me about Northern Ireland—could you explain how come you beautiful, beautiful Irish people fight with each other?" Frank wriggled out of that one smartly, pointing to me, "Ask her. She's living in Belfast." So I gave a mini-lecture on how different American types who hate each other's guts are able to live together because they all trust that they have access to jobs and justice, and all Northern Ireland needs is reformed institutions that would inspire the same trust, because the people there don't have to like each other either, all they have to do is co-exist. While I was delivering this message, a distinguished Irish chef was making green soup right there in front of the camera. "How's Luke?" she whispered to me when I paused for breath off camera. Oh, we had a friend in common! Frank and I were beginning to really get into the singing. She joined in too, as far as I remember. We'd have stayed there singing till the cows came home if the show hadn't ended in a welter of shamrocks, cops, flags, soup, and marching bands. I went out weak with laughter, to be taken to an airport to fly off on a tour to start the selling of the book that had begun on my kitchen table.

That show was a wonderful way to enter the great continent of North America. The kitsch was a liberation: it was like coming out of an Ireland leached of its malice and into some bright place where identity is a matter for lighthearted celebration, not bitter division. My memoir began its existence in a Georgian drawing room in Dublin, at the writing class I went to. The idea for its first words came in a room of classic proportions under a ceiling of intricate plasterwork, paid for in its day like everything else in Ascendancy houses by the toil of Irish peasants on distant estates—

people like my own ancestors who never saw an elegant room from one end of their lives to the other. Well, here I was going out into America, where my story at least started on level terms with everyone else's story. I had as much chance of making it as anyone.

The girl from the publicity department was waiting outside with a limo, which impressed me greatly—this was the first limo of my life. The driver held the door open and I stepped into the back, and with that action, my father came back to me as fully as if he were standing there on the sidewalk. Every afternoon, outside our house, his driver opened the door of his car for him and held it till he got in. So. I was escaping, like him, at last. Chauffeur-driven like he was, when he escaped the tension and chaos of the family home, when he escaped the demands of his children, when he escaped the sorrow and resentment and the smell of drink from his wife and escaped her and our judgment. Like him, I set my face toward the public world. The TV makeup on my face was cracked with laughter as I, too, went off to work.

CHAPTER THREE

Joseph

THE SUN SETS SLOW AND LATE IN THE
northwest corner of Ireland, and often, as it does, gusts of
light, summer rain sweep in from the Atlantic and scour
the wide main street of the village. But the weather doesn't
interfere with Saturday night's pleasure. The street is maybe
two hundred yards long and every few houses there's a pub,
and they glow bright in the dusk as people spill out one
door and laugh and shriek as they jump puddles and run to
wherever they're going next. There are fires, too; even in
July. These are family pubs where the wife will bring out a
bucket of coal, and the kids of the house might do their
homework at a table at the back of the bar, and if you ask for
a cup of coffee, a teenager, maybe, brings a tray from the
kitchen. It isn't cold. The wind the rain rides in on is warm.
The fires are as much a tradition as anything else, like the

musicians—fiddlers, mainly—who come in to the pubs at weekends from small farmhouses behind unkempt hedges at the end of grassy lanes or from lone cottages in a stand of two or three gnarled trees out on the bog. They do their shopping in the grocery stores on the street and then they go to Mass and then they take their pint to the back of a pub to other musicians and at some point, wordlessly, they all begin to play. Over the evening the place fills up. By midnight you can hardly hear the diddly-eye-dye-dye for the din of talk and people calling for drinks across the backs of the men who huddle along the bar beneath the TV screen, mute picture madly animated.

Joseph was one of the men on the bar stools. He had the county accent, which—I'd said to my friend earlier in the evening—was Scottish but flattened by self-pity. We were staying near the village for a few nights on a mission, to hang out until she accidentally, as it were, bumped into a former boyfriend. Now she and the boyfriend had heads touching in talk across the room and I was trying to order a glass of wine, and I said a few laughing words to the man because I was pushed into his chest as people passed glasses and money over our heads. He was an ordinary-looking man, older than I, silver-haired, with an impassive face and a deep, slow voice. He was a man like my grandfather, like any grandfather—settled and laconic. He seemed such a normal part of this rural pub that it was a surprise when he said he was only passing through—he was from a town on the other side of the county. He'd been delivering a load of barbed wire locally. He was a driver, apparently, doing any job that came up.

"Did you know barbed wire was invented by a nun?" I said. But he wasn't a modern man, fluent at banter.

"I saw you often on television," he said. "I always thought, Now there's a girl I wouldn't mind taking home with me."

"*Girl.*" I smiled at him.

I'd had more than enough to drink so we chatted for a while and then I waved to my friend and left. I had high heels on, I remember, and a thin summer dress, and the wind tried to bowl me down the street to where I'd parked in the dark entrance to a field.

IN AMERICA, they screen the windows against bugs. I can't see properly through the mesh, so this morning I took the front screen down and curled up on the bed in the hot sun, with the lake a cobalt blue through the pine trees and Mimmo the dog asleep at my feet. I opened the packet of Joseph's letters. I'm glad I had the bright day and the dog. Going back has its risks. God knows I longed for these notes when I was absorbed in that affair, before I had the burden of thinking about it. He sent so few that when one came to Dublin or Clare or one of my Manhattan addresses, I'd save it unopened for days and days. I'd make myself do such-and-such an amount of work—write two opinion columns, maybe, or draft a whole scene of the novel—before I'd allow myself to open the envelope. Even then I might only peek. Yet this morning I couldn't remember anything in particular he'd ever written. When I spilled the pages out on the bed, I got an almost physical shock at the sight of the short, wavering lines, blotty and ill-spelled, in the curlicued hand of a man, now elderly, who had left school at eleven, the ballpoint dug into scraps of paper. It was as if I never saw them in full light before. I began to wonder whether in spite of our impassioned attempts we ever really communicated at all. Words meant so much more to him than they did to me.

> *My thoughts always go back to the First night I saw you standing on the roadside beside your car. As the lorry lights danced on your body and the dress moved in tune. The wind pulling @ the hedges all I could think of was my Body doing the same with you. At last it come through our body's were made for each other they can go to the Moon, Mars and any were in outer space. But you are my everything always. My hand is burning with the things my heart and my head want to say.*

That was months after, of course.

JOSEPH

.   .   .

I MUST HAVE KNOWN something with a hidden part of me, because I dropped into the same pub the next night and he was there and I drank far too much with him and he drove me back to my hotel. I remember the look of the road, black and rising toward me in the headlights, at one point where a bad swerve startled me into sobriety. I remember a split-second flash of being on a bed and him rearing down on me and whispering to himself, "Oh, you're lovely." When I woke up, alone, late in the morning, it was remotely exciting that he had used a word I hadn't heard in a long time—"lovely"—and used it not to seduce, but in involuntary exclamation. I was so hungover that I couldn't really feel anything and went straight to the shower. In that flash of memory, he had seemed to be making love to me, but I couldn't tell from my body whether he had or not. I could understand why he had gone to bed with me; he'd mentioned three or four times that I'd been on television, looking at me half-frowning as if someone who has been on television deserves a rare scrutiny. But as for why I went to bed with him . . . Oh, well, I said to myself. Anyone who has racketed around as much as I have, and drunk as much, is familiar with the wry, practical action of putting a one-night stand to the side. The only exceptional thing about this one was that it was the first in a very long time.

. . .

HE NEVER DID, in the four and a half years I was mad
about him, remember how to spell my name. Not even
"Nuala." But he did find my address in the Dublin phone
book, and a few weeks after that night he called my house.
Typical of him, it turned out to be, to wait that long before
doing something. He used the least possible words in that
gruff old voice to ask whether he might come around; he
didn't specify when. Weeks later, he turned up. He sat on
one side of the room and I on the other, and if Molly hadn't
been asleep on the hearthrug, prompting him into a few
sentences about a dog he'd had when he was a child, we
might never have thought of a subject of conversation. He
had a formidable capacity for staying silent, for one thing,
and he also gave off a kind of patriarchal disapproval, just as
my grandfather had. I didn't feel I could cross-question
him. He wore no wedding ring; that was the only clue I had
about his private life. The tension in the room grew and
grew till I could stand it no longer, and given that the only
thing we had ever done together was go to bed, I looked
down at my feet and asked him whether he had it in mind
to go to bed. He said something to the effect that he supposed he did.

We made our stiff way upstairs, not looking at each
other. And in the bed, nothing happened.

"I'm on medication for a bit of a heart problem," he murmured. "I'm afraid it must have a bad effect on—"

We were lying beside each other naked, yet neither of us would have spoken the name of the organ on which it had had the bad effect. But the failure to make love made us friendly, and we went to sleep like children.

And then sometime in the night I woke into an unfamiliar feeling of luxury, and as I remembered where I was and that I was lying with my back turned to him, I realized that he was stroking me—that his heavy hand was curving down the contour of my side, slowly, shoulder to calf, and then lifting to start at the shoulder again. Over and over. The movement had a rhythm to it—clearly he'd been stroking me while I was asleep. That thought sent heat through me—that he'd been doing it for himself, not to win something from me. I abandoned myself completely to his savoring of me.

As I write that line I awaken the whole of the moment when I began to respond to him—the feel of the bed rising slightly toward its edge in front of me, the nearness of the wall to my face, his heaviness against my back, the drag of the sensual swoon on the flesh of my face, pulling my lips apart. I borrowed the sensations for the novel I began to write sometime later. "Deep down, under my pubic bone," the heroine says about her first night with the character I called Shay, "it was as if black tar gave a first, thick bubble." And two years after that, when the novel was published, I bumped into Nell on a Dublin street. I'd sent her a proof copy of the novel but she hadn't responded. Now she snapped at me that she hadn't made any comment on the book because it was so bad that it was embarrassing. But, she allowed, it did have one good line.

"What line?"

"That one about the bubble of black tar."

I MET JOSEPH when I was still going on with my journalist's life in Ireland as if nothing had been changed by the memoir coming out. In fact, I was working harder than before, because I'd moved for *The Irish Times* to Belfast. The publishing furor in Ireland was over, but *Are You Somebody?* did very, very well in the United States. It got onto *The New York Times* best-seller list, which was an amazing achievement. In America, if you have a success like that you build on it, so the idea of writing a novel was now floated by a few publishing people I met in Manhattan. I had a fragment of an idea, which my friend Luke had put my way; I had the transcript of a Victorian divorce case, where Marianne Talbot, a gentry lady and an Anglo-Irish landlord's wife, was found guilty of committing adultery with a common Irish servant in and around her husband's mansion in the closing years of the famine decade, the 1840s. But I had very little confidence that I could write a novel, much less an historical one. I would have said I put my creativity into reading, if I'd admitted that I was creative at all.

Trying to write fiction was my central preoccupation during much of the time Joseph and I were together, and his letters must have been an equivalent challenge for him. He could write, though not with any ease. But he couldn't read at all. Or, he couldn't read a book, he said, anymore—the effort made him go instantly asleep. He had once read a novel, long ago when he was a nightwatchman, which I figured out must have been *Cannery Row*. Now, he read only parts of a newspaper, and those laboriously. He hadn't needed to be literate; it was mainly unskilled work he'd done between being sent out to earn what he could as a small boy and now, working for under-the-counter cash after retirement age. I was in the extraordinary position of being able to put things about him in a book, knowing he'd never read them.

But I couldn't dictate what he'd do, or the meaning it might have for me. For example, something crucial happened right at the beginning of our liaison, that very first night when we went to bed but nothing happened and we went asleep, and I woke to feel him stroking me. I've blamed it for starting me off on my four-and-a-half-years' folly. I borrowed it for the novel, of course.

What happened was that Joseph woke me the next morning and we did make love, heart medication or no heart medication. He had a gift for being utterly unhurried. And he wasn't watching me—he was absorbed in the event, and that left me free to be myself. I was more than content when he left me, telling me tenderly to go back to sleep, that he was going downstairs to make me a cup of tea. It had been years at that point in my life since anyone had brought me a cup of tea. I fell back into a trusting sleep, thinking to be woken in a few minutes. But instead, I started into wakefulness hours later in a cold and empty house. He had disappeared.

He did phone, late that evening. He said, "I was afraid that if I didn't leave then, I wouldn't be able to leave at all."

I just cried, sniffing and sobbing along the wires to whatever public phone booth he stood in. I'd been through the phase of wanting to shout at him about equality and that I resented unilateral decisions being made about me, and that I was a human being with thoughts and feelings and he could have consulted me or at least told me about what he planned to do. But I saw afterward that there was an attraction for me in exactly that—the way he'd treated me decisively and selfishly, and not like an equal. I was also alert to the implied passion in what he said, in spite of the gruff way he said it. And that was true all through the time I knew him: that because he was elderly, and a sagacious-seeming man of few words, and after that one sentence, guarded, what he did say had great power over me. Men who are like me talk a lot and use lots of words, but I don't take them quite seriously, any more than I trust my own loquaciousness. But what he said had weight.

I go to a psychoanalyst now, here in America. I've only just started with him so I even do a weekly hour by phone from this house in the summer colony. I lie on the bed and look out into the pine trees and concentrate on our conversation with almost superstitious hope that I'll become a more insightful person, and therefore a more calm one.

I told him about that episode with Joseph.

"So," the analyst said, "it was his tender gesture about the tea that mattered to you?"

"No," I said. "The tender gesture followed by the betrayal. That was the sequence I could not resist."

THE NEXT TIME Joseph rang, I asked whether I could see him—I'd already researched hotels within an easy distance of the town he said he lived in. We met, and fell on each other. And so the thing began. At that point, knowing him was like writing a novel. He told me absolutely nothing except that he drove a truck, so I had to invent him. Because he intimidated me, I made him stand for my grandfather and father and the priests and judges and presidents and other old men who had always run Ireland and the world. So how could he be just a lorry driver? That must be a cover story. Why was he all alone in the world—as he must be, since I listened to every word he said very closely and he never said "we"? Lorry drivers aren't all alone. Why did he come and go without any warning? And then he sent me a postcard of an owl, postmarked Sweden. What would a taciturn Irishman who lived near the border with Northern Ireland be doing in Sweden if not stopping an arms deal or meeting a peace emissary—something secret and important, anyway, in my vague fantasy, and not, of course, harmful.

And wasn't it thrilling that this taciturn old man, leading a life so secret he never talked about it, was crazy about me? And when he trembled because I was in the room, wasn't I subverting the structure of power that had always pressed down on me? Wasn't it like having the patriarchy tremble?

AFTER THE NIGHT he came to my house, I was never with him in one again. Our home was a bed in a room in a motel on a roundabout inside Northern Ireland, behind a busy garage. I don't believe, even, that we ever got under the sheets there. Why would we? We never slept together. He always left abruptly, without apology. He called all the tunes.

He didn't phone, but he wrote, and the letters were where he revealed that he believed himself, as I did, to be in a completely exceptional situation.

> *I now believe in that Christian saying born again. My feeling for you is like the Sea when Moses parted the waters and the people walk across My thoughts and feeling and longing is distilled essences of ever wanting to hold you in my arms. Letting the nectar of your body seal us together. I hope the Sun never sets on our time together. . . .*

In the novel I could do with him what I couldn't do in life. I led my heroine to reject, finally, the Joseph-type man I invented—a character I made much different from the real man. He, I'd learned from the occasional sentences we exchanged about topics in the news, was, in fact, a morose right-winger. But I learned from listening to him that the things he said about gays, and immigrants, and prison being as comfortable as a hotel and too good for car thieves, were things he had to say in his world as well as things he half-believed. Unrewarding work and the world's disrespect had made him what he was, and he was all the more rigid for being an intelligent man trapped in an unintelligent life. He took his information from the men he worked with and from junk media. He didn't know a variety of people. He didn't travel. He didn't have the habit of making compar-

isons or suspending judgment. He hadn't had the opportunity to become a liberal.

All that side of things was irrelevant to our dealings with
each other, anyway. When he summoned me I got into the
car and drove, the car slipping and sliding on frosty roads or
beating through rain or squinting against sun to the motel
room with its big bed, its smaller bed, its floral polyester
covers, its tray of teabags and powdered milk, and its bathroom with too-thin walls which made both of us, I think,
shy. I moved to New York, and longed for the few contacts
he made with me. I moved back to Ireland and waited again,
and whenever the summons came I left the poor dog with
food and water and the radio on, and drove over a hundred
miles through heavy traffic and on bad roads, and paid for
a double room for a night, and waited till he arrived, and
was with him for maybe four hours, at the most, before he
left, and then I started back for home in the middle of the
night. I moved back to Manhattan but went back to this
routine as soon as I was in Ireland again. And so on—more
than four years of it.

I did it for the way I felt on those drives down through
dark Ireland sealed into the warm car, headlights moving
across dead villages, the radio playing softly, sticky again between my aching legs though I'd showered, my nipples
stinging, my face and breasts sore from his stubble. I did it
for the first moment, when he tapped on the door of the

motel room and I opened it not able to breathe, not able to
look at him. I did it for his big, rough hands sliding across
my clothes and my skin, and for the wine he brought for me
and poured into the plastic toothglass, though he had never
drunk wine. I did it because he hardly ever said anything
personal but once he whispered, when I had been ques-
tioning him about his childhood, that it was a long time
since anyone had been interested in listening to him. I did
it for his patience and absorbedness. I did it for the box of
fruit jellies he brought to the room in his holdall every time
and slipped into my mouth as if I were a fledgling and he
was a father bird. I did it because before and during our en-
counters he used to grasp me and hold me tight to his chest
and say, "Are you my little girl? Are you my little girl?" I was
fifty-seven when I met him, and my own father had died
hunched up like a frightened child nearly twenty years
before, but I could not control my response to this man's
fatherliness.

But I wasn't looking around for reasons. Far from having to justify this liaison to myself, I was completely taken
over by it. And so was he.

*Some days I wake up and ask myself is it all a dream. each time
we meet gets better than the last. wanting to hold you ever more,
Closely than the last. At the same time not wanting to hurt you
in any way. Some time if you would cry out, Stop or Do not Stop.*

Oh please let me have all of you. That old story about the lamp
when you rub it you get your wish has some thing to do with us.
How many wishes have you left. Just curl up in my arms and go
back to the womb. I will protect you for ever.

I went back to New York for a second winter. I'd given
him phone cards and he called every so often—again, he
would make no arrangements, so I was always waiting—
and the sound of his slow voice never failed to thrill me.
We never referred, in the phone calls, to what we did when
we met in the motel. We had stilted conversations about
how busy he was at the lorry driving and how cold it was in
New York. When the pip-pip-pip began that meant the
time on the phone card was running out, I'd say at last the
thing I wanted to say.

"Am I your little girl? Am I? Am I?"

Back would come the reply in the judicious tone of the
wise old man I knew by now he was not.

"You're my little girl."

HAVING AN EXPLANATION for things does not rob
them of their power. I could see, of course, what appeared
to be going on. I could see that the obsession with him both
absorbed me and left me free to write. It inducted me into

the world of the novel. There had been long periods in my life when I couldn't have sympathized with a passion like Marianne Talbot's for her servant lover, so alienated was I from my own body, but now my body was the site of the whole of a relationship. That left me with words looking for a home. What we were doing with each other looked carnal, but it was all imagination. There was such a vacuum in our dealings with each other—we couldn't share ideas, or gossip, or talk about our work, we could make no plans, we had never walked down a street together, never shared a meal—that longing rushed to fill the gap. I never knew where he was or what he was doing, and he couldn't imagine where I was or what I was doing. Sometimes there were months when he didn't make contact. He always disappeared completely at Christmas. Three Christmases I spent waiting for him to contact me. He'd get in touch again, maybe in February. I'd make the long drive up to the motel. He outdid his cautious self for me—he'd bring soft candies and put them in my mouth. He'd bring wine and hold the glass for me to drink. But once I was not with him for almost a year. I was healthy and I had money enough for almost anything: I could have gone to Saint Petersburg and seen the snow in the pale nights and the buildings that Vronsky and Anna Karenina knew. I could have gone to a spa and gossiped in the pool with the other women. I could have sent the price of the motel room to children with fly-blown eyes and distended stomachs. And instead, I craved to be with someone who was hardly real. I made a whole side of my life into a desert, as helpless as if I were a teenager completely confused about the emotional and the sexual. The only attempt I made to analyze the situation did go back to adolescence, when I used to watch my mother to find out what these things are. I don't know that she told me in so many words before I was twelve or so, but I know I was still very young when I understood that passion was her touchstone of love, and that she believed that living is hardly worthwhile without passion and that was why she didn't want any of the ordinary kinds of love—ours, for instance, or my father's—either to give or to receive. But I also understood long, long before I had words for it, that the real thing driving her was a loneliness and anxiety from which passion provided her only real relief. It was an existential anxiety, an experience of being unloved by anything in the universe, which I have no doubt she endured, and had no choice but to pass on.

THE NEXT SUMMER, I came to the end of the novel and flew home, longing for what was by now a reliable comfort. I'd saved his latest note to read on the plane.

To my dear little Girl, I reach across the water to imbrace you even for a moment. All this travel you are doing makes me feel everyone is having your time and company you just might forget about me and take the easy way out with all these people wining and dining you fancie hotels. I may just look old hat. May our kisses burn us into one. Hurry Home . . .

We arrived in the motel car park at the same time and walked in together. A busload of women from the Republic who had been at the supermarket nearby, taking advantage of the cheaper prices of groceries and drink in Northern Ireland, were in a coach that was drawing out. One of them—he told me when he finally phoned me—was his daughter-in-law. She had gone straight to his wife.

He was not just cold but defensive, as if I had attacked his family all by myself. His wife wasn't well. She'd taken to her bed. The daughter-in-law was helping him to look after her but they still had to get the doctor sometimes. His wife had always had a problem with her digestion and she could hardly swallow a thing. He was in the doghouse. He'd be in touch if and when he could—

"But—"

"But what?"

I meant, Where's all that stuff that was in the letters? I meant, *What about me?*

"We're worried about her," he began again, piously.

"Actually," I said stiffly, "I didn't know you were married. I'm a women's libber, as you've often said, and I wouldn't—"

"You knew," he said harshly.

AND I HAD KNOWN, though he had never told me. Never given a clue. I'd known not from anything obvious, like the secrecy of our affair; I somehow knew he had a wife from his worn, clean underwear. And I knew he was a father from the complacent way he issued pieces of advice—advice about my car, advice about the weather. You could feel the privilege that was extended to him in his home, that had made him so lordly.

IN A FEW MONTHS he phoned me again. He couldn't live without me. That was the moment when I should have pulled the tatters of principle around me. If he was a supposedly happily married family man, then he was the first in my life I'd ever had an affair with. It is an evidently wrong thing to do—for one woman to use her freedoms to secretly steal from a woman who is less free. I had thought myself an outsider to the domestic life but wholesome in my way, not doing anybody any harm, not a shabby adventuress. I felt real solidarity with the wife, too, now that his pattern of unexplained absences and returns was revealed as simple cheating on both of us, at his convenience. I was making a fool of a truckdriver's wife, even as I was treated as somebody of worth at arts festivals in Melbourne and Charlottesville and Gothenburg and spoke to applause in Miami and Providence and Treviso and all over the place. Even as I thoroughly enjoyed the acquaintance, in New York, of people as variously talented and smart as Manhattan people are supposed to be. Even though I had the real privilege of staying at Yaddo, where some of the other guests were artists of the finest quality. I was living a new life, rich and rewarding and full of supports. And she, presumably, had no such sources of affirmation, but instead, this man, this husband.

In any event, I behaved as if she didn't exist. I called the best hotel in the county town of his county. They had only a suite available; I paid for the suite. We started again. And now that he was released to do so, he talked about his wife and family all the time. He loved to boast about her—what his boss had said about her cooking, what the teacher in the son's school had once said about the way she helped with homework, what she herself had said admiringly to him when he got the coffeebar manager to change the sandwiches she didn't like. He loved to bring her presence into a room where I was, because I was difficult, but she had been his reassuring familiar for forty years. I saw that she was the kind of woman he liked and admired and that he didn't actually like my kind, and that by now it was making him uneasy that he couldn't place what I was doing with him. I had need of him, but he had no need of me, I saw in his sideways looks at me. He started to talk about heart problems—breathlessness, pain. He was nervous about the hours on the bed, though they were more langorous now than anything else. Once I drove all the way to the motel at his command, but he neither turned up nor phoned, and I saw that I wasn't quite as hurt as I might have been. I had wanted to live with the authenticity and insouciance I attributed to Colette. And here I was. A common cheat, and not even much wanted.

YOU DON'T SOUND WELL, I said to him when he rang after a silence of six months, and he said no, he was fine, but maybe the line was bad, he was calling from Portugal. Portugal! Yes. He and his wife had sold their bungalow and bought a place in an apartment complex somewhere between Faro airport and the sea. He was hoping to get informal driving work, but the Portuguese policemen were in cahoots with the Portuguese drivers. The climate was lovely and he was feeling great and they had no intention of coming back to rainy Ireland.

I'd always known that the other woman isn't told more than she needs to know, but all the same, this was amazing. What about the grandchildren they were supposed to live for? What about how they were supposed to be simple and unsophisticated people who wouldn't dream of living abroad? What about *me?*

So, goodbye, he said.

HE DIDN'T STAY away from me. He called me on my birthday. My sixty-first. I had looked up the name of a hotel in what seemed to be a seaside village near where his apartment must be. I told him I'd be in that hotel on the First of May. May Day.

"Contact me in the Hotel Sol," I said, and I wouldn't let him make any comment, because I knew he'd want to stop me.

I WISH I hadn't gone. I wish the whole thing had ended when I was told about the wife. Or at least that it had ended in the motel with an embrace. But in real life, the mock-heroic is a lot more common than the heroic. And what I got was less, even, than that.

I flew out for a week on a charter trip and got a cab for the long journey to the Sol, which turned out to be in an undeveloped, almost remote spot, though it was only about twenty miles from where Joseph lived. It was a simple, concrete bar with rooms, run by a man who didn't speak English, right on the sand of the beach. I took a room for a week, and unpacked my books, and went down and had a coffee on a deck above green waves. I began to relax. There was only a narrow, iron bed with a plastic-covered thin mattress in the room, and the walls were speckled with dead insects, but Joseph and I would manage. I needed bottled water and sunblock, so I walked up the narrow road past groves of rustling palm and eucalyptus to the supermarket on the main road, stopping over and over to look at the white birds in the mudflats of a small lagoon. Egrets, I thought. How wonderful it was going to be—a whole week, with him only thirty minutes away!

But when I got to the checkout of the supermarket I discovered that my purse had been stolen. Every bit of money I had had was in there, unless I'd left my credit card in the pocket of my other pants. I prayed all the way back to the Sol. Yes, thank God I had the card, so if the owner would trust me I could get room and food. But I had no cash at all and no way of getting any. There wasn't a police station in the place, and what help could the police be anyway? The one bank branch didn't speak English and wouldn't lend me cash on the credit card, and I didn't know the PIN to use at an ATM. I'd need cash to get a cab back to the airport. And I was imprisoned, effectively, not able to get a bus to the town or make a call from the public phone that was the only phone, or buy fruit or stamps or an English newspaper. In any case, I always panicked completely if I had no money in my pocket.

He came to the Hotel Sol after two endless days and nights, but he didn't have any money on him. I understood from his sullenness that his wife was in charge of even petty cash. But he had some hidden, he said, and as soon as he could, he'd bring me that. Meanwhile we went to the room with the smears of dead mosquitoes on the walls and the soft, repeating crash of the waves outside. I could hear a wheeze deep in his chest as he talked. We could not be playful. And what had ended our play wasn't even anything to do with our personalities—it was fatigue, it was his turn inward, listening to his own body in fear. The animal in him had become a small and fearful thing, and what he was doing was crouching over it, conserving its faltering vitality. None of this was said. He managed a parody version of what he had been. I never even thought of criticizing him. Anyway—what him? The him I knew was gone.

The last I saw of Joseph was in the white heat of the next afternoon, halfway up the old road to the main road, where I'd walked, aimlessly, and was looking through a mesh fence at the birds in the mud. He drew up in his small car. He looked great, tanned, in a baseball cap, but he didn't get out or even turn the engine off. He just handed me the money out the window and said he'd be back when he could. The equivalent of forty dollars, it was. But he did not come back. There were four more days and I spent most of them wondering bitterly whether he'd chosen not to come back or been prevented from coming back, until eventually I saw that it didn't matter. It didn't matter. He was a separate person with a separate life, so separate that I couldn't even repay the money. I did not know his address, which I couldn't write to anyway because of his wife.

I DON'T KNOW whether he's dead or not—there's no way I could know. Today I sat in the sunny window above the lake, wondering whether to keep the packet of his letters or throw them away. I don't like thinking about him, after all. It would be pointless to regret knowing him, though I still wish it hadn't happened. But I'd need to hate him to burn his letters. They're a great achievement of his. I wish I could give them to someone of his own—like returning the medals he won to a hero's family, I might say, if it weren't an analogy that begins yet again a slide toward unreality. What hero? He wasn't a hero, and I was a disgrace to myself. Yet, I see something of the heroic about what I never call our relationship. We were both grabbing at life. We took risks as big as the most famous lovers did, so as to live.

WHEN I LOOK at the Joseph affair, and how long it lasted and how many other options it prevented, and how much it must have hurt his wife, the first thing I see is my own greed. And then, as usual—though this is an explanation, not an excuse—I see the wretched influence of my mother. But it was also something to do with writing.

Sometimes people ask me how to write a book, and the question gets my best attempt at an answer because it comes from a serious part of the questioner—people have dreams, more or less wistful, of a self-expression that life has not so far allowed them. But the way a fiction is made is basically a mystery. Are connections made between body and mind, for example, during the conjuring up of a story? Have the memories out of which a fiction is made been laid down as much in the physical self as the mental? It seems to me that before I could start inventing my story, my unconscious self led me to two enabling decisions, both of which took phys-ical form. One was to leave Ireland to do the actual writing in Manhattan. And the other began that night in the pub in the rainswept village, to the sound of fiddles, when I met Joseph. I used him; but, you know, I paid for it, in not being known by him. Since he didn't read books he didn't, of course, read the novel I did write, and I take it he doesn't know that there's a character in it who takes his false teeth out the better to kiss the heroine's breasts. Joseph knows the person who was caressed by him like that, but he doesn't know the person who wrote it down.

I called the novel *My Dream of You,* which is a phrase with multiple resonances in a poem by Montale. But I meant something quite simple by it. There are love objects we simply dream up. They are not real people to us; they are the embodiment of a dream. We unleash both want and need onto them, and while we're dreaming, we believe that they can fill up the bottomless pit where want and need are endlessly renewed.

CHAPTER FOUR

Public and Private

IT WAS A CAVERNOUS ROMAN CATHOLIC
church of the old-fashioned kind, the kind I'd known as a
child, bright with gilding and stained glass and glossy tiles.
The priest, in a robe of cream and gold, walked to the pul-
pit and bent into the microphone. He looked gravely at our
congregation.

"What are we to do?" he began, in a low, urgent voice.
"What are we to do?"

I had hurried across the wintry streets to this monastery
in a Republican area of Belfast, and now I leaned forward,
yearning to hear what comfort the father-figure up there on
the altar might give. I'm not what Catholics mean by a be-
liever, and it was a long time since I'd deferred to pro-
nouncements from pulpits. But I was lonely and nervous
after a few weeks living in the city, and I longed for the

priest to gather me in. It was the beginning of 1998, when individual Catholics going about their ordinary business—a taxi driver, a pizza delivery boy, a man working underneath a car in a backstreet garage—were being murdered every few days, presumably by a loyalist gang, for no other reason than that they were Catholic. The war in working-class Belfast had come down to plain, neighborly hatred. It was a relief when the dead body I saw one evening a hundred yards from my own front door turned out to be not the latest in the sectarian sequence but something to do with drug dealing.

It makes you seek protection very quickly when the community identified by the religion of your childhood is being terrorized. The killers had revealed that their slogan was ACAT—Any Catholic will do. I was a Catholic, if only by culture, and I'd come here to huddle with Catholics. I had always known churches exactly like this one, places where part of you could be serious, part of you as casual as if you were strolling around a piazza. I was familiar to the point of indifference with Irish Catholic worship. It was a revelation to discover that the familiarity could mean so much to me now—that the slow rhythm of the unfolding of the Mass, the Confiteor, the Kyrie, the reading from the Gospel, could be such a consolation.

The priest began the sermon. "What are we to do?" he asked again.

At least I was part of the question, even if the answer he arrived at—that we should put our trust in God—left me out again.

I'D GONE to Belfast in a lighthearted frame of mind. The success of *Are You Somebody?* in Ireland was long over and it hadn't yet come out in the United States. I had nothing going on in my professional life when the editor of *The Irish Times* said to me that the war in Northern Ireland was winding down, and that maybe as part of treating the place as if it were normal I should move there and write my opinion column from there. The North had always seemed exciting when I'd visited it for a few days to make a quick television program or write a short piece, but as far as daily life went, Belfast had a reputation for being as charmless a place as there is in the First World. An acquaintance who was a pastor there told me that a worried parishioner asked for advice on whether it was all right with God for the canary to have a swing in his cage on a Sunday—that kind of place. But I had no personal life in Dublin; I had only to put the dog and the cat in the car and I could move in a day. And the drive to the motel where I had my meetings with Joseph would be much shorter. And anyway, it was a good idea. Everyone who went to Northern Ireland wrote about the Troubles or the politics and economics behind the Troubles. It was quite original to assume that there were aspects of the place which were no more or less than mildly interesting. And I felt that it would be a blow for a commonsense way—a woman's way—of looking at the place, to emphasize the perfectly comfortable lives that most of the people of the province lived most of the time. I took a bit of pleasure, even, in annoying the local media prima donnas who would hate to have it pointed out that not everything to do with their situation was utterly exceptional, which is what domesticating a corner of Northern coverage would certainly do.

It was so unusual for a Dublin journalist to set up house in Belfast voluntarily that I was an item on a popular Northern Ireland television show, which brought me fifty or so letters from viewers who wanted me to come and see how blameless their lives were. Which I did—a journalist who is not going to meet people through drinking in bars or through the other parents at a child's school or through colleagues in a workplace has to take what routes into a new experience present themselves. I had pleasant cups of tea and made my choice from trolleys of exquisitely prepared savories and scones and cakes in many spotless Northern homes. Hospitality is so competitive there, especially among Protestant hostesses, that I came to expect that there'd be sliced grapes in the cream cheese finger sandwiches. Person after person explained to me that they themselves weren't bigots and that everyone in their locality had always got on fine until the Troubles inexplicably started. It would be possible, of course, to feel contempt for people entirely oblivious of the power structure within which they had their own security. But what do people in general know about how their privileges relate to their fellow citizens' lack of privileges? Is it possible, even, to live with an exact knowledge of where you yourself stand in the network of human exploitation? I used to feel real sympathy, backing away from this or that immaculate bungalow, for the husband and wife waving from the neat porch. Imagine people so hurt at the portrayal of their native place that they must ask a passing journalist to tea and bombard her with anxious propaganda! It is one of the small, collateral losses of a conflict like the Northern Ireland one that the name of the place becomes a synonym for bad news. The war had taken away these people's pride in where they were from, and you could feel that that was a building brick taken from their lives.

YOU WOULD THINK, seeing me sipping tea on sofas, that my sense of Northern Irish life would be biased toward innocuousness. But from almost the beginning I realized that no matter what my editor said, no one in Belfast itself thought normality was setting in. My first day, a low, winter day, I went to see a gate lodge to rent, tucked behind grandiose granite pillars at the end of a village—a single street above the pebble shore of a gray sea channel. The skeletal beech trees around the house had been contorted by winds from the east. "I wouldn't if I were you," the estate agent murmured. "Not when you'll be going back there late at night by yourself. . . ." And true, there were anti-Catholic graffiti all over the pillars, and the curbstones were painted red, white, and blue. So I settled for a vaguely mock-Tudor terrace house in a "mixed" part of Belfast which was intended, from its dandelion-choked front garden to its concrete backyard, for transients. I hated knowing there was a bedroom with a bare-mattressed bed on either side of the tiny back room where I slept. The empty rooms meant that though I had persistent fantasies of somehow getting Joseph there and playing house with him, in fact the place was nothing like a home. No one ever came there, and the silence was all the more acute because trains went by behind and buses in front. Molly never colonized the place. When we came in she went straight up the stairs and slunk in under the bed. But though I pitied the dog, I had to keep her with me because she was all the company I had. I used to marvel at how completely a personable and competent person, namely me, speaking her own language, not a hundred miles from where she was born, could be so complete an outsider.

I didn't understand the culture of the place well enough to sketch my speciality—the small picture. I had never had any trouble in the Republic finding things to write about. Anything might be grist to my mill (I could easily spend a thousand words thinking out loud about a phrase like that). Politics, current affairs, movies, accents, scandals, who wore what at the Oscars, why Iran is not a horrible place, a manager harassing a young woman on a corporate weekend break and then firing her, consultant doctors accepting gifts from patients anxious to skip waiting lists, racist assumptions in reporting on places like, say, Croatia, why Irish Catholics didn't get upset at Scorsese's *Temptation of Christ* when Irish-American Catholics did, whether there is any hope of getting European farmers to consider the consumer, why the internationalism of the new young is more apparent than real. I swam in my home culture like a fish, and with thorough enjoyment. But in Belfast I couldn't read simple clues. The chatty woman in the newspaper shop, for instance, answered every "Good morning!" except mine. "Of course not," a local remarked to me months later. "You buy *The Irish Times*."

THERE WERE wonderful moments, but the place was so damaged by years and years of suspicion that none of the moments lasted long. The rich Protestant ladies shopped for Saint Laurent and Escada in boutiques that had sprung up in a semiderelict slum area for the simple reason that it was a Protestant area and the ladies felt safe. I was looking through the clothes on a rack listening appreciatively to the almost indescribable smugness of their chat when the saleswoman asked could she help me. "I'm just browsing, thank you," I said. They heard my southern accent. Not one more word was said by anybody and as soon as possible the place emptied. It wasn't that they thought I was a terrorist; it was that they knew I was a stranger. Next day, I happened to drive up to the northeast corner of the island, whose natural beauty is almost unspoiled because development has been arrested by the kind of warfare the place knew—an intimate kind, not a matter of battlefields but of a bomb at a wedding reception, a lethal tripwire across a country road, a street cleaner murdered as he sat in the back of his van eating an apple. I met a family who ran a camping ground on an emerald hillside that sloped down to a seashore of cliffs and caves and rocky islets. I walked the little lanes around their place on the sunny winter day, the waves below me bouncing and lacy with foam in the breeze. Blue hills dotted with white sheep stretched away to a headland and the air was freshness and lightness itself. But there is a limit to the consolations of nature. Where I was walking was represented at Westminster, re-elected every time with a huge popular vote, by a virulent anti-Catholic who had done as much harm to the wider community in his lifetime as any political figure. A few miles away was one of the villages where vicious, animal hatred displayed itself as soon as the young men started drinking on the day the Protestants had their annual procession to commemorate becoming top dog, back in 1690. A local woman had just told me that though the children waited together at that shelter—there where sheep were cropping the turf—for the bus that took them to schools in the nearby town, they didn't speak. Catholic and Protestant children, lovely, neat, intelligent children, didn't speak to each other at all. Or again, Protestant teenagers couldn't go to the really cool disco because everyone knew the IRA ran that particular roadhouse. I stopped to look at glossy blackbirds pecking along behind the grazing sheep, and when I turned back, the road had noiselessly filled with a file of British soldiers creeping along under the hedge in camouflage gear, their rifles cocked.

In Belfast, at the end of a day like that, I might loll on the synthetic velvet of the blue sofa and watch the tops of buses and lorries and army trucks go past against a changing sky above the half-curtain. I don't understand this place, I'd say to myself. I don't believe anyone who offers to help me understand it, either. Every bit of confidence, which had seemed so secure at the time of the success of *Are You Somebody?*, fell away from me. I'd take the dog, then, and throw sticks for her in one of the municipal parks, all bandstands and regimented marigolds and asters from the days when this was a respectable industrial town. Or I'd take her to the grounds of the huge, plastic leisure center where she sniffed happily among the detritus left by kids hanging out behind the shrubs to drink and smoke. Or we'd go down the dreary road to the supermarket and buy something for a meal. Then I might push the plate aside on the table and try to start a column.

I BROUGHT A FOLDER with those columns from Belfast here, to this room in the summer colony near the Delaware. I thought they might remind me of what that three quarters of a year was like, if I tried to write about it. But they don't bring back at all, in fact, the baffled, self-doubting person I know I was when I wrote them. They're good: they're full of information and quirky thought and feeling, and they add up to a picture of a strange but interesting place, whose state is well caught by the unstable point of view of the columnist. But then I never did understand how the private me, the reporter, brought back what I wrote, the report. Africa, the Philippines, Israel, Poland, Iran, and many other places—I turned my experiences there into interviews and analyses and feature articles, but those are not what is imprinted on my enduring self. What I remember is the feel of panic because there were no taxis and the airport was closing, or because the immigration guys probably wanted a bribe but I didn't know how to bribe here, or because while I seemed to be listening to some government spokesman, I'd just felt in my pocket and my passport wasn't there, or because there was someone moving in the bushes outside the bedroom windows . . .

The cost of taking hold of the opportunities life offered me seemed never to get less. I had enough self-belief to start off along any tightrope but not enough to get to the other side without beginning to falter. When I was twenty-four and at Oxford, the University Dramatic Society was important because its annual production was reviewed by the London critics. Anyone could offer to direct whatever play they wanted, but to be chosen as that year's director you had to get through a stiff interview. I got through, because I could talk very persuasively. But what did I think I was doing, taking on theater production on a semiprofessional level? I didn't have the skills. That became obvious, and it humiliates me still to admit it. Ten years later I had hardly improved. I could give examples of all kinds of exotic settings I worked in that were blurred for me by panic. I was in Florence for the first time, during short, gray, midwinter days, collecting photographs of documents and artworks for a BBC educational film about a Renaissance festival. I didn't know how to use a public phone, or say a few sentences in Italian, or get things notarized, or drive a car. I had a room in an old *pensione* with a bulb so dim I had to stand on the bed to read, which made me laugh, but when I went out about my business I could hardly swallow for nervousness. That time, I was bailed out by a splendid American woman who knew her way around the Florentine bureaucracy. I remember her vividly—the tall, confident way she walked in her flowing fur coat, and how her little son had invented a private language of his own called Truesh—a variant on Truth, I suppose—and how W. H. Auden, who was a friend of the family, was working on a dictionary of Truesh with the child, and how she'd gone around as a young woman with Shelley Winters and how she stood at a bar drinking a coffee and looked at me incredulously and said, "You've *never* been married?" I came back with the material I'd gone to Italy to get, thanks to her. But it is the feel of her sweet-and-sour personality, half-kind, half-impatient, that lives in me as the main thing I learned on that trip. Florence itself was an almost irrelevant backdrop to my anxieties. I took hardly any notice of its ancient power or made any response to its beauty. I was just one of the people scurrying against icy winds across squares of old brick and stone, past statuary and domes and roofs etched with snow. After darkness fell, I was at a loss, eating every night in the Chinese restaurant while I read an English newspaper by the dim nightlights. I wasn't confident enough to be adventurous by myself. Intrepid explorers often come from a socially privileged background; the rest of us have to learn how to make our way in strange places step by nervous step.

And I didn't give myself a chance. I remember, from the many times I got myself to a wonderful place, and got myself there in the role I wanted—that is, doing a job, not as a tourist—and then failed to take full advantage of it, a stay in the American Colony Hotel in Jerusalem. I was making a program about the monotheistic religions that coexist in that city, a humble educational film, though no easier to put together than any other bit of television, especially with a crew of young Israeli thugs who treated our Muslim participants with casual aggression. In the center of the old hotel there were small courtyards, and there, in the warm, starry night lit by lamps and with the smell of exotic plants filling the air, a British foreign correspondent held court every night. I remember drinking my wine like a mouse in the corner while he, a big, good-looking, self-satisfied man, in a freshly pressed designer djellaba made of finest lawn, clapped his hands for mint tea and talked nonstop about his exciting life to his admiring coterie. I thought, watching him with a mixture of contempt and wistfulness, "It is impossible that the truth of the situations he covers can filter through such vanity and excess." The next night he was there again, and I was there in my corner, drinking a little too much wine. And the next night, again drinking maybe a little bit too much. I sat there preening myself on how fine and uncolonial my sensibilities were compared to his, but it was I who was almost out of my depth with my project. The same streak of arrogance that got me involved in doing difficult things kept me from seeing simple truths about myself, though you'd think my shaking hands would have reminded me of my mother. The whole middle of my life I never slept without pills, I drank too much, and I was alternately remote from men and reckless about them. I used the same props as she, though she had nine children and an evasive husband, and I had an enviable job and need not have had a care in the world.

It took decades to learn how to talk myself into believing, every time I went out to do a job, that I would not fail. I was a television producer who suffered agonies of panic in the control room but could do the rest of the job very well. I could neither leave difficult jobs nor be happy in them. It was only after I wrote *Are You Somebody?* and it was a success that the side of me that confidently leads me on became just a little stronger than the side that undermines the confidence and drags me back. Yet none of this conscious struggle, which has been the central experience of my working life, is suggested in my journalism.

I found journalism hard, like a relationship that is always hampered by misunderstandings. My columns from Northern Ireland pass muster perfectly well, but they're filtered through my limitations, just as the foreign correspondent's were through his. I know this, but the public never could. I was always made uneasy by the three-way relationship between the journalist, the situation written about, and the reader who believes that what he's reading is somehow a neutral account of the situation. Perhaps a need for greater truthfulness built up within me. I know it was a liberation to turn to the relative honesty of memoir and, then, fiction. A lot of the journalists I've known have been working on other kinds of writing and it's assumed that this is because working with words is their field, but I think it's because even the best journalism is emotionally unsatisfying. The conventions of journalism are oppressive to the honest self.

"WHERE WERE YOU WHEN . . . ?" Some public events are so big that we mark them by where we were when they intruded on us. Where were you when—when JFK was assassinated, it used to be; now it's where were you when the planes flew into the twin towers. But even much smaller public events are remembered by those involved in terms of their intersection with the personal life. For journalists covering Northern Ireland—for anyone who cared about Northern Ireland—the final cliff-hanging hours of negotiation of the Good Friday Agreement were momentous in that way. The wait for news was carried live from Belfast on Irish television. The Agreement, the first comprehensive peace settlement proposed for the province, is a brilliant, institutional cat's cradle, designed to allow the Catholic and

Protestant communities parity of esteem, which was woven by diplomats and civil servants and politicians over many years and brought to the table by the energy of the Clinton administration. But local malice could easily and would gladly have stopped it there.

During that afternoon I was playing with Joseph on the bed in the motel we always used, my private life continuing on its own way, just as the farmer goes on plowing and the horse goes on scratching itself in the Breughel painting as Icarus plunges from the sky. All the rooms in our home were the same. Two beds with a foot of space between, one upright chair and a huge television set, and a small, plastic bathroom not more than three paces from the bed. I'd bought new underwear during the week in a daze of anticipation of ecstatic pastimes that involved being half-dressed rather than naked. Now, the loudness of the soundtrack of the TV commentary invited us to be more abandoned than ever, and on one level, the afternoon was about sliding again and again down slopes of sensuality. But I was listening to every word from the television set, and though my body was soft and slick, my mind was increasingly dry as the meeting in Belfast went on and on, and anxiety mounted that no deal could be swung. I knew that it was near-miraculous to have every party to the cruel old conflict around the same table, and I knew that if this effort didn't succeed we were further back than square one, with less hope than ever of release from the sterile and degrading repetition of Anglo-Irish grievance. I was writing about it in my head. And all the time, there was the obbligato accompaniment of gasps and murmurs as Joseph and I excited each other.

He cared about the outcome of this day, too. He knew why, when a presenter almost ran onto camera to say that it was going to be all right, that agreement had just been reached in the conference room behind, I burst into tears. But my impression was that, like the patriarch he was, he'd issue his opinion on political matters to his cronies, perhaps, slowly, late in the evening in the pub, or to his listening family at a meal. He had no zest for discussion. And I wasn't interested in his views anyway, because I'd long ago noticed that they were monotonously pessimistic. The only people I wanted to hear from were other journalists. I wanted the inside story. I could hardly wait for tomorrow's newspapers. Meanwhile, there were peaks and valleys of sensation yet to traverse before he hauled himself off the bed with the usual mumble about having to go. It was an afternoon of being fully alive, that one, though I don't know whether I'd think of it with such pleasure if the Agreement were not still just about in place.

I had more hope than belief. Everything *about* the situation has been changed by the Agreement, I thought, not everything *in* it—it is not a resolution of difference but a structure within which difference might possibly be managed. I knew that if you were a Republican with a developed view of the rightness of getting England out of Northern Ireland, or if you were a loyalist with a similar argument for keeping England in, you'd hate the Agreement. But journalists find themselves with middle positions because they have, as part of their job, shared the experience of people on every side of the conflict. The actual combatants, of course, Republican or loyalist, out there in battered housing estates or behind the hedges of remote fields, moving arms, laying fuses, lying in wait for their enemies, couldn't care less what someone like me thought—but then again, no one much cared about them, trapped by the accident of birth into lives both damaged and damaging, and then written off, when the power brokers arrived at the conference table.

I hid my doubts about top-down solutions. I remember that a CNN film crew stood me against a wall and Christiane Amanpour asked me whether I thought the Agreement would bring peace.

"The media will disappear from Northern Ireland," I said cheerfully, or words to that effect. "This has been a conflict that never suffered from neglect, the last of the English-language wars, and one of the few conveniently placed for airports and hotels. Now—well, Ireland's exceptional days are over, and the whole place is set to become as dull as, say, the Netherlands. The Agreement will take a while to stick, but it will stick. It's all tied up. In Washington and Dublin and London and Brussels—they've thought of everything."

I was being flippant so as to give the appearance of conviction, because I wanted to be convinced. I wrote columns for newspapers all over the world praising the Agreement, and my own column in *The Irish Times* was a strong supporter. I often remembered looking up at the priest yearningly that time at the beginning of the year when I was so afraid, and how true to itself that wintry Belfast full of foreboding had seemed, and how ready to settle forever into blackness. So I praised the Agreement every place and time I could. But I don't know how media people are ever sure of their grasp of events, or know that they haven't simply preferred peace now to a more distant and difficult justice. For myself, I'd been on my first book tour in America just before the Good Friday of the Agreement—the tour that began with the hilarious Saint Patrick's Day party on *Good Morning America*—and I had glimpsed the New World. The experience made me want even more to burst free of the old ways we were stuck in, Ireland and me. I could see that there was liberation on offer there to people who have had so much of suffering that they've given up asking what it is for.

. . .

THREE MONTHS AFTER the Agreement, I stood on trampled, muddy grass on a breeze-block housing estate on the edge of a small Northern Irish town, in the pungent odor of a still-burning house. Charred, drenched wood. Melted paint and plastic. Singed clothing. Perhaps—the whole body recoils—roasted flesh. This had been a mixed estate of not very fortunate people. The local Protestant hoods had of late been intimidating the last few Catholic families to get them out. The night before, they had torched this house, with three small boys inside.

The piece I wrote began:

There's one good thing about losing three lovely little fellows to fire. At least their belongings are gone too. At least there's no home left that would have the shapes of their small lives imprinted on it. There are only the burned walls, and the gaping window-spaces. The people who loved Richard and Mark and Jason—such carefully nonsectarian names!—will not have to see the boys' shoes or their toys or any of the things that would bring the reality of them back. There is nothing left. It is better not to think that they were real, warm, squirming boys. Because the neighbors heard them screaming as they were—the voice cracks at the two words— burned alive.

I continued: *If neighbors they can be called*...

Because the neighbors, of course, either set the fire themselves or knew who did. I stood there looking at those neighbors at their front doors, as they in turn watched with closed faces the outsiders like me gathered, uselessly, in front of the burned house on grass made slick with mud by the firemen's hoses. I was overcome once and for all by the sheer dreariness and sadness of this place and of the province all around. Listening to those little boys screaming as they were consumed by the flames was by no means the worst thing a community did during the Northern Ireland Troubles. But it went to my heart.

TOWARD THE END of 1998, I asked the editor of *The Irish Times* for indefinite, unpaid leave of absence from my job. I arranged to leave my dear dog, Molly, with friends on a farm. And with the money I'd made from *Are You Somebody?* I moved to Manhattan for three months to try to start the novel that various people connected with publishing had mentioned to me—as if it was the most natural thing in the world to expect a 58-year-old who had never written a word of fiction to be able to write one. I set off, one of many millions of Irish people to have made the east-west journey, in pursuit of that particular miracle. And I found once again,

in Manhattan, that the teeterings on the tightrope of failure
at least make you flexible. I'd been there five or six times,
making programs for the BBC or Irish television, or, once,
on a State Department tour for international journalists
the year Bush and Dukakis disputed the presidency. But I'd
always stayed in hotels and moved around by cab. I didn't
know how to make a call from a public phone or how to use
the subway or how to get what I wanted in a pizza place or
how to contact Directory Assistance. I didn't know you
can't buy a bottle of wine in New York on a Sunday. I didn't
bother reading *The New York Times* because it seemed to me
badly designed and decorous to a fault. Anyway, this time I
was so lonely that I searched out the Irish newspapers on
stands, to touch their pages as I read. I knew that I was
nothing like an immigrant—that I had acquaintances and
money and was basically a seasoned traveler. But I didn't
feel like that—I felt as if I had never survived anything, I
felt as insecure as if I was back in one of the many places I
thought I'd never conquer.

I lived at the beginning, while I stumbled toward the
start of a novel, in an underground room behind the kitchen
of a Mexican restaurant—a man coughing himself to death
upstairs, a mattress on planks on the floor, the dim light
coming down at a slant through barred windows. The only
thing was, that room and my loneliness within it paradoxi-
cally gave me a sense of belonging. I was one with all peo-

ple who have uprooted themselves and journeyed to a new place. The Jews of Central Europe trying to say their names to the officers at Ellis Island; the Kurds I saw working as dishwashers and toilet cleaners in Greece for a few cents an hour; the old Russian prostitute I met on a bus in Toronto who didn't have enough English to judge whether the men she went with were safe; the Irish-speaking Irish, back when they built the canals and railroads of the English-speaking world, losing their community as they moved into the language of the overseers; the Iraqis waiting on desolate islands off Australia in hopes of working their way into comprehension of a culture where even the alphabet is a mystery. The whole world is vibrant with the heroism of people who have had to start anew, and Manhattan is the greatest of all the cities created by such people.

THE SINGLE most surprising thing to do with writing happened to me in that room. On the day I started writing fiction, the very day, I slept, naturally, for a whole night. Then again, the next night. Then again . . . I couldn't believe the miracle—which still happens, and still astonishes me— because I had been a settled insomniac since my teens. I suppose it could have been coincidence, and that some hormone shifted around in my aging body and happened to grant me sleep on that day. But I prefer to believe that, re-

leased at last from fact, I was able to be truthful. Something
like that, anyway. What happened was like a dream—I contemplate it, knowing there is significance to it, but I can't
explain it.

Sleep was a new source of energy, and so was what
flowed into me from the streets. Partly it's the fact that you
feel a citizen from the minute you start living in New York,
whereas in the old European cities no amount of residence
can earn you the privilege of belonging. And partly it's the
stimulus of the variety of skin color and language. I might
see, maybe opposite me on the subway, an illustration of
the melting pot—flat, Andean-Indian features beside a
beaded skullcap from Baluchistan beside Chinese, Hispanic,
African-American people, Russian people, Fijians, Haitians,
Nepalese, a Hasid, children in little blue jeans and sneakers,
on this knee or that. And it's partly that you feel you can
grasp the place, that it isn't hidden from its people, that the
whole of Manhattan's urban experience is there to be seen,
from the snaggle-toothed graveyard down at the bottom of
Broadway or the brick of the Ear Inn, a few yards from
where the West Side Highway must cover old wharves, to
the smooth façade of the houses that were there in Washington Square when Henry James was writing *Washington
Square*. You can see and touch the history of the place since
the bow of the first boat from Europe scraped ashore and
the native people melted back along their paths through the

scrub. The old synagogues and churches and warehouses and factories, the faded advertising stencils high on the sides of buildings, the carved names of forgotten mutual-help societies, the palimpsest of the city's history where a banking hall became a lighting showroom which became a Buddhist temple, or a vaudeville theater became a cinema which became a fitness center, or the general stores of the Jewish community became caves lined with counterfeit designer purses—all is spread out before you. The city's histories are inscribed on it. And I read there a welcome to hope and hard work that was the opposite of what I knew in fatalistic Ireland. Manhattan is full of buildings that are wonderfully improbable to look at but perfectly sturdy, and similarly the feel of the city, of people effortfully rising or precipitously falling, is alive with momentum, but not unstable.

I made a start on the novel and then I went back to Ireland for a while, and when I returned, the next winter, I got a better room—a ground-floor studio looking into trees. The boiler was underneath my floor so I used to wear a cotton nightie all day. I got my own little black cat from the FurryFrendz animal shelter. The novel was inching forward and I sat in the hot room with the roar of traffic from Houston Street in the distance, trying to write, with the radio tuned to the classical music station. I waited for Joseph to phone. I signed up in a sports center to learn how to swim. If I hadn't been so lonely, I would have been very, very happy, and as it was, I was happy.

THERE WAS A LONG, low loft near where I lived, open day and night, on the top floor of an old office building, and it is divided into cubicles, each with a desk and a chair and a lamp and a mat for lying on the floor. It is called the Writers Room. My place was often uncomfortable, so I took out a night membership, and several times on freezing winter nights I walked up to the Room. And I'd see, passing along behind the New York University buildings where there are heating grids, the huddles that are the sleeping places of the homeless. Then there'd be more people under snow-blown cardboard and plastic in the doorways along Broadway. That was a dreadfully cold period, and most of the homeless would have been in shelters except that Mayor Giuliani was taking advantage of the weather to sweep the shelters, serving old writs on offenders who had evaded earlier writ servers. At five o'clock in the morning as I made my way up Broadway, there was no one else in the deserted city but the snow-covered ones and me. I could not but compare our lives. And a sense of the savagery of the fate of the losers in this great city came up with me to the Writers Room. I couldn't accept that I should be cozy in the comfortable loft with its kitchen, its reference library, its lockers for my things, should be treated so carefully, just because I called myself a writer. So I used the Writers Room maybe four times in all, each time more self-conscious about naming myself a writer.

Perhaps this was a reaction to the change from being a journalist—journalists don't expect special treatment, for one thing. But what was mainly disturbing me was writing an invented story drawing on my emotional and sexual sensibilities—on my private experience—whereas for many years commenting on public facts had been my métier. I had to struggle with the conviction that what I was doing was of no consequence at all—baby stuff—whereas writing about something like the homeless would have been some kind of action. I had lost what had made me useful—my access to a newspaper readership.

I identified with those who found the city, as I had found so many places, harsh and indifferent, even though I was now snug and safe. I could not train myself into accepting my enormous privileges. *Are You Somebody?* couldn't have got a better welcome in the United States than it did, but my inner self was familiar only with places of not-belonging.

DURING MY last winter stay, in 2000, I lived in yet a third place, a sublet on a high floor on the southwest corner of

Washington Square. I finished the novel there. I used to sit at the window and watch the marvelous weather play over the low-roofed plains of SoHo and Tribeca that stretch as far as the southern curve of the island, where tall buildings made a semicircular palisade from Wall Street across to the definitive, authoritative towers of the World Trade Center. Snow used to dance below the window. Great misty skeins of rain moved majestically across. And sometimes my interior sunshine found a counterpart in reality, and there'd be a day of wonderful cold brightness, and corners of glass and mirror would flicker and wink here and there in the cityscape, like fireflies.

"It is closing time in the gardens of the west. . . ." They say the summers before the First World War in Europe were particularly beautiful, and looked back at through the deluge of war they must have seemed so. I know my Manhattan, before its innocence was torn from it, was most wonderfully enriching. My diary entries for those three stays do often say "lonely" or "very lonely," but in retrospect the loneliness has fallen away and I think of myself as having been welcomed by a city never stingy with its gifts. I never dreamed that my battered old heart could become so light. I remember a morning that might have been any of those lovely mornings, hurrying along Mercer Street on the way back from the swimming pool, hurrying because the air was cold—though to a person used to the Atlantic's

damps, an invigorating, dry cold. I'd nearly managed to
swim, too, that morning, head down in my goggles, body
rolling, arms slicing, or intending to slice, at any rate, the
water ahead, and my body felt fine after the exercise. Under
my arm I had a fresh loaf of crusty bread from Bruno Bakery. In ten minutes there'd be a range of other pleasures—
my New York Times spread out, my pot of tea brewed,
WQXR on the radio, bread and butter and jam on the table
and Cobweb the little cat down beside my foot eating his
breakfast at his bowl as I ate mine. Nothing to do all day but
bend my sentences this way and that. The life of a queen.
Everything, every single thing about it unimaginable when
I came in from that dark street to crouch in the church in
Belfast.

THE TOWERS of the World Trade Center were my famil-
iars when I lived on the seventeenth floor of the Washington Square building. They may have looked bland to people
who only glanced at them, or peered up at them from below,
but I knew them as neighbors. I knew them adrift with
cloud and I knew them with their city of windows gleaming through evening rain and I knew them dull with cold in
that iron weather before snow breaks out. I had actually
walked every foot of their perimeter, and I wrote about that
in a memorial piece, the week after September 11th.

There was a notice in the bookshop at the foot of the World Trade Center building one day—a man who'd written a book on the birds of Manhattan would lead a birdwatching tour from there, All Welcome. The ten or so of us who showed up were a typically motley, eccentric, socially inexplicable group of New Yorkers. One old man had a solar tepee on, and some of the others wore sturdy shoes and carried binoculars, though we were following the walkways and piazzas directly under the towers, and looking for our birds in the plantings in pebbledash troughs and dank beds that divided the expanses of concrete. Several of the birdwatchers had water bottles fixed to their belts, though I don't suppose we were ever more than a hundred yards from refreshments. But the repartee was loud and funny, and as we mooched along toward Battery Park we actually did see more than a dozen different kinds of bird pecking at the thin grass, or going about their bird lives under the municipal laurel bushes, behind the roller skaters and cyclists and baby buggies and the courting couples entwined on graffiti-covered benches.

"What bird," someone asked, "is the official bird of New York?"

No one was sure.

"It should be the bluebird," a woman said dreamily, "because the bluebird is the bird of happiness."

"Don't you believe it, honey," a woman in full makeup, wearing a long lace dress and a huge backpack, said. "No one ever came to this city to be happy."

In September 2001, some of my sisters and their partners and I were on holiday in Italy—the second Italian holiday of our lives. We were staying in various places on the
lagoon south of Venice, when those towers were hit. I was
in a hot Internet café in Chioggia, surrounded by the noise
of teenaged boys playing video games when I went online
and saw the image of the plane striking the side of the first
tower. I thought it was a video-game image. I didn't understand. Out on a low island, some of the others were staying in a village house, a horrible place of banging shutters,
steep, linoleum-covered stairs, high, musty beds. We sat in
the dark interior room in front of the old television set and
tried to understand together. We could get picture and
sound as the set warmed up, but after five minutes or so we
lost the picture and we couldn't follow the excited Italian
commentary. We'd turn off the set and let it cool down and
then start again. There was only one public phone on the island, and I had only a few units left on my card. I rang the
office in Dublin. An overworked newsdesk was very short
with me.

There was always a wind blowing across that low island,
rattling windows, blowing gray sand across the road. We
went back to the television set. The old ladies who lived on
the island shook their heads when we tried to share the
shock and said, *"Male, male."* Bad, bad. We didn't know anyone who was missing but we knew people who did; our

niece, Deirdre's daughter, earlier in the summer had worked for a very nice rich man in his house in the Hamptons. Deirdre called home with one of the last units. The man was missing, presumed dead. His brother—missing and presumed dead, too. It was Tuesday when the attacks happened, and our vigil went on intermittently through Wednesday and Thursday. Friday was to be the day of mourning. At midday we walked down to the chapel in the village to join the prayers. But we were the only people there.

I DIDN'T FORMALLY LEAVE *The Irish Times* for another six months or so, but I finished with it in any real sense, then, on 9/11. I made my way back to Dublin through airports crammed with stranded Americans reduced by events to the condition of all the powerless, displaced people on the planet. An advance opinion column I had left behind with the newspaper—a jocose piece about a local thing— had been run on the Saturday after the atrocity in my space, because none of the production editors thought to drop it, and because I hadn't made the effort to go home early and insist it be dropped. It is hard to convey the professional chagrin at seeing a grossly inappropriate piece under your byline at such a time. And simultaneously, I saw very clearly that it didn't matter at all. Comment had reached new levels of inadequacy. My public role had dissolved away.

. . .

THERE IS AN IMAGE that lives, vivid and detailed, in my head. It is of a hillside in Zimbabwe, in Africa, on the morning of an election day. It was very cold in the mist, and polling wouldn't start for another hour or so, yet snaking along through the huts and then diagonally up the hill, and then along the ridge, was an orderly line of citizens, in their car-tire sandals, their patched rags of sweaters, their old woolly caps, their hand-me-down coats, holding children by the hand and with babies on their backs, all waiting patiently to exercise, in the relative privacy of the booth, the privilege of the franchise. These were people whom colonizers had treated like subhumans, whose war of independence had often descended to savagery and whose governance was more and more questionable. But the basic democratic idea of the secret ballot was there too, and the idea that every person has a political role and is of civic worth. To me, that hillside shines with the dignity our public selves can have.

And then there's the opposite. I always thought of what was done on September 11th as half-private—as having to do with huge, personal envy of America. Envy, which is hatred and desire mixed; not just hatred. I thought that on one level of his being, the terrorist squad's leader, Mohammad Atta, had seen in America what I saw—its openness, its capacity for new life, its sweet, naïve optimism, its denial of the past in the interest of the widest possible future. I thought that something in the soul of this man, who was still sitting on his mother's knee when he was eighteen years old, could not bear that a place of such freedom could exist. When I did write about September 11th, the dream I was grieving was only a notch away from his—an outsider's dream, an immigrant's dream.

Like everyone else, I brought my own private experience of grief to the grief of America. I understood when I went back to Manhattan and stood at the site of the ruined towers that hatred and envy, as much as loss and sorrow, unite us. They are everywhere the same. When I stood there at the Trade Center site, I was standing in the smell of the burned-out house in Northern Ireland where the three little boys perished—thousands of times magnified, but not very different.

CHAPTER FIVE

Responses

IN THE HOUSE WHERE I LIVE IN DUBLIN, there are shelves in the hallway, and on the shelves, near the door—where I could carry it out after I'd rescued the dog if the place went on fire—is a large cardboard carton. There are about five thousand letters from readers in it. About half of them, I'd say, are from generous-hearted people who've written to me simply to send good wishes. But the other half are in one way or another about pain. If there is a God, he must be exhausted by the vigor with which his creatures grasp onto their destiny and try to make it make sense, even to the point of spelling it out to a stranger.

From Australia:
Nuala, my eldest sister hates my father and had the gumption to tell him so on his deathbed, for remaining married to my mother

*and putting us through hell. Thankfully I recognized this early on
in my life and quickly and easily made the choice to be childless. I
cried my eyes out when my father died and partied when my
mother died. She suffered from postpartum depression which
worsened with the birth of each child.*

From an Irish woman in Canada:

*I am a 30-year-old working girl (read sex worker), anyway my
mother who has no knowledge of my occupation gave me your
book. This letter is one of thanks. I can't give a surname or address.
One lives in secrecy in my profession. I can see ten men in a night
but am essentially alone outside of that. The other girls are such
a troubled lot that being with them twelve hours a shift is all the
heartbreak I can take.*

From a man in California:

*I live here with my wife of 58 years. She is 85 and is moving into
ever darkening dementia, as well as other issues of diminishing
states of well-being. My son aged 53 lives here as well. Ten years
ago he suffered a stroke. He cannot find employment due to his loss
of speech.*

From an Irishwoman:

*I lost my virginity to a married man in a concrete hotel. And
then I began to wake up. I was twenty-eight. Reading your affairs
and adventures I felt so angry I lived life as if I had no body.*

From a woman I remember when she was the prettiest girl in one of the schools I went to:

My two marvelous children still bear the scars of living with their father. And me. I was insane in those days and had not one friend in the world. I remember seeing you one day with a guy and you looked so self-possessed.

From Chicago:

My father came to America in 1920. He was a severely melancholic raging alcoholic who beat and abused my brothers and me. My mother, of Irish descent also, was so depressed she stood by and passively watched. For 62 years I have felt profoundly unloved and spent my life looking for love and validation from others, especially men.

From Texas:

I went to confession to a priest who had given me last rites when I had cancer. I did a bald-faced honest grocery-list disclosure of every horrible thing I did—the affairs, sex, etc. I didn't want anyone to know these things about me. He was so forgiving and kind. A few weeks later we had dinner in the cafeteria at work and a few months later he asked me out. He married me. It's been good. You just never know when you are intentionally living your life taking care of yourself and keeping in touch with yourself what happens next.

From Harvard:

Nuala—a friend of mine rang me on Christmas Day. She had just finished a long-term relationship like yourself. Now re-reading I have just got to the point in your book when you spent your first Christmas completely on your own. I realize that at the top of the page I have written 25/12/66 (M). You see, Mary took her own life.

From the Midwest:

My elderly parents still attend Mass every day and have the church which they love more than their children. My mother is still an active alcoholic. My dad quit drinking 45 years ago and turned into a bastard that hates everyone and everything except the Church. I'd like to make some sort of mark on this earth before I'm forced to leave it but I can only make a mark that will soon fade.

From Boston:

The single happiest day of my life was my daughter's wedding. But that night, when the party was over, was the most painful, lonely night of my life—more painful even than the first nights alone in my new apartment right after I'd left my marriage. If my ex-husband hadn't been remarried I think I would have enticed him to come home with me—for just one night.

A mother of five sons:
On a brief visit from my husband he said he was off to search for love and passion. They were his very words. I have not understood them. He had love from me, and still does, and his kids. He is a great artist and musician. Perhaps he wanted passion from me. He has thrown away what most people would die for—a loving family.

From New York:
As an abandoned and unwanted child your book explained for me—finally, at 76 years of age—my inability to keep out of other men's beds as a young woman. Perhaps the violence of your family provided some insight but farmed out as a baby to sweet, Quaker, child-carers, I was totally unprepared for what followed. That in the case of my marriage it meant drink and violence I was simply at a loss to understand. Happily though, I have been blessed with children though my youngest, who had epilepsy, died inexplicably of that condition.

From New Zealand:
I would love to have married someone I both loved and liked. Funnily enough, caring for Mum and the role-reversal that entailed meant that in a sense I did reluctantly become a mother in my fifties. Ironic, isn't it? You've got your cat and dog, I've got my budgie, not a bad pet for a single living alone because he has

*learned to talk so I've got an excuse for talking out loud in an
empty house.*

From Northern Ireland:
*My grandmother and grandfather (housewife and general laborer
respectively) bought a piano for their eldest child, their son, who
showed neither interest nor talent, but my mother was gifted and
could play immediately by ear. However her parents sold the
piano regardless.*

From rural Ireland:
*Why am I writing to you? Shame. My mother is a filthy dirty
person. She hangs pink frilly curtains and paints lime green on a
wall with plaster on it sticks wallpaper up with cellotape, pees in
a bucket in the kitchen though we have two toilets. My mother
used to quote poetry, my father ridiculed learning. There are stories of him putting my older brother in a trailer with a bull he just
bought at a fair, and kicking my sister the full length of a long lane
when she was 11 telling her what a fat arse she had.*

THERE WAS A TIME when I was getting two or three letters of this kind every day and I could hardly believe the parade of human hurt that I was being asked to witness. Hurt
was what the writers of these and many other letters of the
same kind had in common with each other and with the

person they'd met in *Are You Somebody?* because otherwise
they were from very different people in different circumstances. The envelopes, the paper, the handwriting—each
one different. I used to look at the names of the post offices
where they'd been franked—names that were exotic to
me—and try to make some link in my own head between
someone unknown to me standing in that post office, and
myself, sitting in a room in Dublin reading what had been
posted there. It was as if I was forced to do exercise after exercise in the imagining of other people. In that way, the
human response I got to the memoir was the bridge for me
between it and what I wrote next, a novel. Because a memoir is an unpeopled thing. There's just one governing voice
in there, and other people play their parts in that voice, not
their own. Whereas a novel is a village full of distinctive
characters and events, as the letters are.

It isn't identification that's going on here—I am not like
an old man with a senile wife or a Canadian prostitute, and
they know it. Nor are the letters cries for help—the situations described often seem to the writers to be beyond help.
I replied to every single letter I got, and I know from experience how often the advice I suggested sounded ridicu-
lously small. An atmosphere emanated from the letters that
floated in almost poetic detachment from the facts re-
counted in them. The bad things that had happened had
been so complete that they belonged now to the nature of

the writer's life. There was no such thing as a search for practical improvement. The act of writing a letter to a stranger would be an almost floridly impractical way, in fact, of going about improving matters, if that were the goal.

But it isn't. The stranger is, crucially, a writer, and writers are the nearest thing the human community has to spokespeople. Letters from troubled people have no forward impulse. They incline back, toward the state that was there before the bad things happened—they incoherently yearn, and yearning is the note they heard the writer sound, and the arena within which they and the writer are equals. Since this is all unsayable, the letters seem to make no sense. But they do if they are understood as being about losses and voids, things that are not there, and as inhabiting absences and silences. Their emotional integrity is their justification. Their cadences proclaim them members of a secret society, the society of those who have truly suffered.

THERE'S A FUNKY old hotel in downtown San Francisco whose grand, shabby foyer has seen everything. Behind the foyer there's a big cabaret room, windowless but with a ceiling of stained glass. You have to adjust to half-darkness if you push through the curtain and go in there from the ordinary, Saturday-morning street, and adjust even more when you realize a live radio show is going on, and the tall guy in red shoes, Sedge, and his sidekick, vamping on the piano, are entertaining an audience with interviews and musical numbers and anything else that comes into their heads. It's a very laidback, Californian show, and when I went on it to promote my novel, a little fantasy became real. I sang, and an audience sang along with me.

I explained to Sedge when it was my turn to be interviewed that my book hadn't always been called *My Dream of You*—that I'd wanted to use a phrase from an old-fashioned ballad about being in America but homesick for Ireland.

"The song's called 'I'll Take You Home Again, Kathleen,' " I said to him, "and I called the heroine of my book after it—Kathleen. Every Irish person knows that song—mind you, it turns out it was written by someone from Illinois who never set foot in Ireland, but it's one of the great weepies anyway."

"Sing it!" he said.

I can't sing, but I had a go, anyway. I falteringly began, *"I'll take you home again, Kathleen, across the waters wild and wide . . ."*

Gradually the piano came in to lead the melody: *"To where your heart has ever been, since first you were my bonny bride."*

People here and there in the audience were beginning to sing along.

> *"The roses all have left your cheek,*
> *I've watched them fade away and die,*

> *Your voice is soft whene'er you speak,*
> *And tears bedim your loving eye."*

And then I took a deep breath and launched with the melody into the lover's pledge:

"Oh! I will take you back, Kathleen, to where your heart will feel no pain . . ."

By the end of the verse the whole room was singing, and the pianist was throwing in lots of trills, and my cracked, breathy voice was giving it all I've got:

> *"And when the fields are fresh and green,*
> *I will take you to your home, Kathleen."*

We were all helpless with laughter and emotion when I was seen off to terrific applause. You don't often hear such a terrible singer deliver a song with such conviction. But I have always loved that song, no doubt because of the paternal kind of love there is in it, that takes responsibility for returning Kathleen to that ever-powerful place, home. To sing this song helped along by willing strangers, to sing it in San Francisco, to feel the wave of affection and amusement rolling toward me where I stood on the stage clutching the microphone—for all this to happen to me, at the age of sixty-one . . .

What are people responding to? How is it that they so

easily enter the state that the song's sorrowful melody evokes? Kathleen is literally pining away with the longing to go home, to be restored to the mythical homeland which is what Ireland is for many Irish-Americans—and I suppose a lot of the people in the audience were Irish-American because they knew the words. But they didn't want to go anywhere, and the homeland we were all longing for wasn't Ireland. Where they wanted to go was toward me—they could hear a note of commitment in how I sang, for all the clowning, and they wanted to console me by joining in. Big sentimental songs like that one do draw on deep wells of regret. I was fine: I was halfway through a book tour that was a success, and I felt well liked, and capable. I'd enjoyed my interview on the show. But I knew the other side of things— I knew that I was not young, and I knew that there was no one to promise to bring me back to wherever it is that would make my heart feel no pain.

A little line waited afterward in the hotel in San Francisco to shake my hand. Humans seem to need to move towards each other once the dimension of the imagination has been opened up. Though what, specifically, had been imagined as we sang, would be impossible to say.

I DON'T THINK it was the precise themes of my memoir that provoked response, though family pain, and midlife disappointment and ever more anxious hope, and love searched for in vain, are states that have meaning for people across every difference of age and gender and culture, and across geographical distances. But I think it matters a great deal that it happened to be my mother who caused me the most pain in my life and who is the one person I've known who refuses to die completely, even buried at the crossroads with a stake through her heart. I notice that in the extracts from letters I've reprinted here—taken at random from the first few hundred of thousands received—mothers and motherhood figure as sources of pain. The fact that it was our mother who wouldn't allow us to mean anything to her, that it was our mother who gave us daily proof of as much dissatisfaction with her lot as if she'd been a queen sold into slavery, opened my feelings in the memoir to all comers. If I had had the same to say about my father, it would have been much less spacious a field. What there is to say about fathers is specific, but what there is to say about mothers is easily generalized.

But just as important, I think, in evoking a response, is that I genuinely understand so little about my life. I have only the most tentative explanations for anything I ever did or didn't do. And this unfinished understanding of myself leaves room for the reader to join me, to project something of themselves. I think there is a subtext to my book—and to many contemporary confessional books— that is not verbal, but rhythmic, and readers graft their own emotions and experiences onto that rhythm beneath the overt text. I felt it myself, once and once only, when I overheard myself reading *Are You Somebody?* on the radio and in the split-second before I realized who it was, responded myself to the notes in my own voice.

It is not what you have but what you have lost that links the reader and the writer. The longing to repair loss is in the rhythm and tone of the written piece, not in its words. The rhythm is where the reader senses the writer's truthfulness, as unerringly, I think, as an infant senses whether the person who is holding it loves it. The writer and the reader are always singing along together, both confident of the tune, but the writer more certain of the words than the reader. I understand what people are saying in their letters to me no more or less well than they understand me. I might say, What am I supposed to do with the sorrows people have confided in me? But isn't it the same thing as I want them to do with my sorrows, published to them? Don't do anything for me but know about me, be with me. You know this song too, don't you? Well, won't you help me sing it?

SOME OF MY letter-writers said this with ardor:

"By now you can tell that I not only fell in love with the book but with the author as well. There is so much I want to know about you. Just you. I would never ask more." "If I had been one of the lucky ones that you desired I would never have let you go. I would have proposed marriage in a New York minute." "I want to meet you. Years ago I stayed in Dublin. Perhaps I passed you on the street." "I am ready to come to Ireland for a visit but not without an invitation and a date when you would be available for a 'date.' I propose that we would meet for dinner and then, if miraculously we were to hit it off, spend half the night talking and afterward decide separately whether we have a desire to do the same or similar again." "I'm happy I got to know you, and this letter is probably as much knowing as each of us needs. Besides, I couldn't afford sudden flights across the Atlantic or long-distance phone calls." "You would be most welcome to stay with me. I have a quiet, comfortable home to myself in which the loving presence of my children still lingers." "I could come up to Dublin to meet you for a day—I have a dog and could not leave him for any longer." "Spending one hour with you, perhaps on one of your walks, would mean a lot to me. I could meet you any-place in the U.S. or on a trip to Ireland. If you didn't like me I guess it would be a wasted hour of your life, but if you did, it could be the beginning of a friendship, or per-haps more."

.　　.　　.

THE NOVEL I WROTE, *My Dream of You,* even in its title claims a place in that same realm. I see now that it is about the imagination, and the inventing of a love object in the same way but on a much larger scale than those letterwriters invented me. And it is full of speechlessness, just as the relationship between me and the letterwriters is speechless. It is also about a woman, Kathleen, who doesn't love herself and who is the daughter of a woman who didn't love herself. This was my point of departure when I began Kathleen's story—two years to the day after I changed my life by going on the Irish television chat show to talk about *Are You Somebody?* I drew up my chair to the table in the dim basement room in Manhattan where the man somewhere above coughed and coughed. I wrote the first few words and then went to the top of the page and typed in *Ad Majorem Dei Gloriam*—not that I was dedicating my work to a specific god but that I wanted to note that trying to write a novel was a solemn undertaking for me. I knew hardly anyone in New York back then, and when I went out to get a pizza slice or a Chinese meal I was as nervous about the streets and as lonely as if I were a poor immigrant. I missed Ireland terribly. I missed my little dog. But I suppose the distance I put between me and any life of my own helped me imagine

Kathleen—Kathleen, a woman who might have written me a letter, so certainly is she one of the connoisseurs of loss and yearning. At least—she is, at the beginning of the novel.

I didn't have any plan. I just made the plot up, with immense difficulty, as I went along. I knew I wanted Kathleen's modern story, that of a fifty-year-old travel writer whose life has ceased to satisfy her, to relate to the *true* story of the Victorian Anglo-Irish landlord's wife who was first incarcerated and then divorced because she had an adulterous affair with one of the servants. I wanted to use the historical material I had on that affair if only because it was full of social detail, whereas I was brought up on a version of Irish history that was heavily male, with the emphasis on wounded pride and insurrection. But I didn't know what kind of English I could write the historical parts in. Obviously, people didn't speak in the past the way we speak now, but I don't believe they spoke prithee-sirrah-unhand me, either. There was the further twist that the adulteress, a member of the ruling class, would have spoken only English, whereas the servant might well have spoken only Irish. So, how did they communicate? But, I thought one day, millions of couples don't communicate, even when they speak the same language. And suddenly I saw that that's what the heroines could have in common; they could both be the sort of woman who rushes recklessly toward the promise of passion, not wanting speech with their lovers, not valuing communication—not valuing any other state except the occasional stratospheric high amid the long, dull low of the most extreme choice.

It took me a while to realize why this theme, of all the themes in the world, seemed privileged to me. It does exist—I've known both men and women who are living as intensely as in a Racine drama. A woman, for example, that I met in Belfast, an ultra-respectable headmistress, moved there thirty years ago and stayed, though she loathes the place, for love of an even more respectable public figure, someone big in one of the Protestant churches, whose secret mistress she is. But where the theme came from was— Step forward, Mother! My mother saw herself as a martyr to passion. My mother believed, and told me a hundred times if she told me once, that the ten years of romantic bliss she had with my father before things went wrong were more than almost any other woman got, and more or less justified her existence. What she was with the rest of her and for the rest of the time was a nothingness she just had to put up with, stoically, escaping into a book or a drunken daze as quickly as she could. Those absorbed, irresponsible, egoless, time-blurred states were the nearest she could come, I suppose, to the nirvana she had known. My actual mother wasn't in my mind when I was trying to invent the novel, or not much more than usual. But the shape of the thing—loving passionately and then almost as passionately paying in long, grieving aimlessness for the passion—I knew from her.

THE ONLY THING IS—that's not how Kathleen turned out. The very fact that I didn't know where I was going with the fiction, and had to keep myself open to constant imaginings, led me to write in the end a quite different book from the one I began. This is the glory of fiction compared to the memoir, and the reason, it occurs to me, why one could readily imagine reading nothing but novels but not nothing but memoirs. A memoir is only about what is already known. For all the play you can have with it, the plot is known in advance. But anything might have become of Kathleen.

And when it did, I found something in myself that I hadn't known was there. The story of Kathleen dramatizes the point of turnaround in my own life. I was the tragic person to whom the letters were written. But I became the ordinary mixture of a person, not tragic at all, who did her best to answer them.

What happened was this. I constructed the story. I led the plot toward the offer that would keep Kathleen tied to Ireland and waiting for Shay, the perfect lover she has met. The Tristan and Isolde offer. The scorched earth offer. If she will be his secret lover, always in readiness for his visits—

and he won't be able to give much notice of when he can
visit—the reward will be a love affair so intense that it will
be out of this world. I could see it—a house in a wood somewhere, and a room golden with light and warmth, and a
lover driving dark roads fast, completely intent on the
woman waiting in the radiant room. I don't think I myself,
most of my life, would have been able to turn down such an
offer. I wouldn't have weighed what the loss of family and
friends and community and work would mean. I would
have believed, rightly or wrongly, that I could live perfectly
happily on books and the natural world and the company of
animals, as long as somebody drove toward me as alight with
purpose as Kathleen's lover swore to her he would be.

Kathleen was meant to assent to this. That was the
whole point—that she and the landlord's wife would both
end up buried away for the sake of a dream of love. But as I
wrote the scenes of the plot, I discovered that under my
own hands, Kathleen was changing. At first I thought the
reason was technical. People in novels are always doing
things; something has to happen on every page before you
can get to the back cover. So much more, in fact, has to happen to fictional characters than happens in real life that
their development is enormously accelerated. Kathleen
never stops doing this or that, whereas in real life I lolled
around or went to bed early or walked up to Macy's and
tried clothes on. You can't put that in a novel—"Did noth-

ing all day today. Read an old copy of *People* someone left on
the subway." Kathleen's sheer busyness was the first thing
that made her incompatible with the passivity of the role I
had planned for her. And I kept giving her tactile activities,
which fought against the abstraction of passion. She gets
her hair done, and she keeps near to Spot, the dog, and she
carries a baby down the garden to look at ducks, and she eats
well, and she watches the wild cats play in the field, and she
collects little bits of dried gorse to start the turf fire in her
cottage. These acts provide her with repeated small sources
of vitality. I also started connecting her to her past. She goes
back to her hometown, for instance, after thirty years away,
and spends the night in her brother and sister-in-law's
home. She shares a bed with her little niece and falls asleep
listening to her brother calling the cat in downstairs. The
feel of the child came from the times when my little blonde
niece used to visit from London, and lie beside me on the
bed in my slum house in Dublin as the light faded from the
sky. The cat I gave the same name to as the cat of a man I
loved when I was a troubled young woman and we were
trying with no success to be partners—Furriskey, he was
called. I was connecting to my own past, I see now, in tiny
acts of redemption. I could have used details like these in
any way—as emblems, for instance, of lost happiness. But I
used them to illustrate reconciliation and warm content.

So what happened to Kathleen wasn't just a by-product of the making of a fiction. I was changing, myself, in symbiosis with my heroine. Happiness—or if not happiness, a robust vision of how to manage its absence and live well—had crept up on me. It subverted my character's fatalistic progress toward self-immolation. It became not in character for Kathleen to live for love alone. She had become too widely life-loving to ruin her own life, even for honest passion perfectly expressed. I led her more and more slowly toward the scene where her lover puts the proposition to her. And when I got there, in a complete reversal of what I had set out to do, instead of saying yes to him, she leaves him an elegant message—not using words but a song—that tells him no. She didn't want to turn into my mother.

EVEN WHILE I was rescuing Kathleen, I myself was marooned in the relationship with Joseph.

He'd phone from Ireland every few weeks.

"Is that my little girl?" the low, slow, old man's voice would say. My inner self would soften and began to spill, heavy, like candlewax.

"How's the book going?"

Usually I'd say that I was struggling and it was rubbish and I couldn't see that I'd ever be able to do it.

"Well," he'd say, "if we didn't have the bad days, we couldn't have the good."

"And how are you, Joseph?"

"Fine, fine. And yourself, otherwise?"

"Oh, fine."

"Okay. Well, I have to go now. I think someone wants to get in to this phone box."

"Joseph—"

"What?"

"Nothing."

"Well, goodbye now."

"Goodbye."

Then I might cry out, "Ring soon again! Don't leave it so long! Joseph, you haven't rung for three weeks—"

"Got to go now. Be a good girl, and get that work done!"

Joseph was nothing but a voice that said words and, very occasionally, his words in a letter, where the energy of his dream of me broke through the labored, unpracticed hand-writing. Letters and other messages from men and women who'd read *Are You Somebody?* were still catching up with me. Sometimes they told me stories that were like novels and sometimes stories that were like journalism and sometimes the words carried a vision of me that the writers had made up, the way one makes up a story. All day I worked with the words under my typing fingers, and the ones I chose both affected the rest of my life and were affected by it. So if I say

I lived with nothing but words, I don't mean that my life was empty. Far from it—my silent room was filled with a busy traffic of communication.

I WAS TEN YEARS OLDER than the fictional Kathleen. Ten years makes a huge difference when the tunnel of time leading forward is narrowing. By the time I finished *My Dream of You* I was living in the sublet on Washington Square. The weather was very, very cold and I came down from my eyrie only once a day, to get the newspaper and something for a meal in Balducci's and to gesture to the poor, frozen boy from the Korean grocer to follow me up to the apartment with logs—the fake logs they use in the city that crumble away to an unpleasant kerosene-smelling ash. I had no social life. A bit of talking on the phone; a lot of music on CD, and on Sundays, Lincoln Center—by myself—for live music. The book I was writing was full of grass and soft rain and children and kissing, but I knew nobody who was entitled even to reach across and touch my hand. I went to the opera by myself, and to the Cloisters and the Statue of Liberty and I went alone down to Key West to Hemingway's house and stayed in an "adult resort" where the women had wrinkled throats but youthful, round breasts that stood up by themselves even when the women were sunbathing on their backs, and I visited a mangrove swamp and swam and ate Cuban food, always alone. And when I went back to Ireland I was alone in the cottage in Clare, and the solitary Christmases and New Years were stacking up; three, four, five . . . It was nothing like as easy for me as it was for Kathleen to crawl out from under a weight of fatalism.

Yet by instinct I was doing for myself what I did for Kathleen. I began to multiply small sources of well-being in my daily life even though the big sources of well-being hadn't opened up for me. And if I sketch here the things that made me happier than I'd been for many years, and that I proffered when I could to the grief of the letterwriters, I do it knowing how banal those things are. I don't believe that life offers us many consolations of the same size and weight as it offers us hurts. But we can patch things over with what life does offer. Or—it seemed to me that I could. I believe in all the common nostrums that every magazine article peddles: Friendship, travel, art, animals, the natural world. That's all there is. They are not love itself but they are nurturing, the way being loved is. The difficulty for the grief-stricken is taking the first step toward them, but anyone can take that step—only being sick in body or mind cuts off all access to them.

That, or abject poverty. It requires a special effort to live a healing life without some money, and this is so obvious to me that I couldn't understand why the letterwriters never mentioned money. Is it that they all have enough? Is it that they think money is irrelevant to suffering? If so, they're wrong. My mother, my father, and almost all of my brothers and sisters and generations of Irish men and women lived lesser lives because of a shortage of money. My own fate as a young woman was shaped by a shortage of money. I took the decision for Kathleen that she would have enough money not to worry about it throughout *My Dream of You,* because I didn't either, by the time I was her age. Middle-aged people do eventually catch up with as much money as they need. I had a plan for getting old, that I had worked out before I made money from *Are You Somebody?,* that I knew I could afford. I was going to sell my Dublin house, and with the proceeds and the old-age pension, I'd have enough for years in the cottage in Clare. I was going to live with as many dogs and cats as came my way, and I was going to read and listen to music and drink wine. I had certain things lined up for those quiet years. I've got the CDs of Wagner's *Ring* to study, for example, and the works of William Faulkner and *Don Quixote.* I was going to go back to my efforts to learn to play bridge. I wasn't going to need much money for any of that, even the wine. My parents died in their sixties, so I took it for granted I wouldn't be around for a prolonged old age. But if I did become infirm—well, our Aunt Ann is paid for in her home for seniors by the Health Board because she has no money at all. I could sell

Clare and when that money was gone I'd have nothing either, and I'd be looked after, too. Of course, the kind of old
folks' home I'd be likely to end up in would be awful, but I
never thought about that. I was like a teenaged girl who believes she won't get pregnant because the alternative is too
awful to contemplate.

Spend money on living, I would always say, except that
some sad people are made sadder if they can't think of anything they want. My tone, talking about money, is always
wrong, anyway. I don't lie, but I find it hard to strike the
note of truth. Money is such a private thing. One's relationship with it is full of hidden depths and shallows. I gave
some of mine away, and I also spent it—spending is also a
way of spreading money around. My luxury items, like my
Himalayan cat or Frette sheets or getting my teeth done by
the most expensive dentist who is also the most gentle, feed
back into the economy in the form of wages in catfood factories and bales of cotton bought at auction in Egypt and
the salary of the receptionist who calls to remind me of my
appointment. So I understand, at any rate—there should
be a book for people like me who've never had more than
about a thousand dollars in disposable income called *How to
Manage Money Even Though You're Afraid of It and Think You Don't
Deserve It*. I tried to invest. A girl I met when I was taking
bridge lessons said put it in the stock market and I did, but

this summer of 2002, when it began to matter to me to know where I stood, I rang up the accountant and he said, "You don't want to know, Nuala. You just don't want to know." The market may rise again, of course.

I also now own a small place in Dublin that I bought for my brother who drinks, whose hair is going gray, though he is the second-youngest of the nine of us. He lived in a town in England for no reason except that an after-care agency once put him there. When he was a small boy he used to fish in Dublin Bay and I thought if he came back he might fish again, and also that there is nowhere on earth, probably, as accepting as Dublin of men who, like him, are barely clinging on. But what did I know about his real life? Because I thought it must be bleak and lonely, was it bleak and lonely? If you are not already delicate about what is owed to other people's autonomy, then coming into money is liable to make you worse.

My big venture was to pay in full in advance for a space in a warehouse in lower Manhattan. The plan was that someday, if nothing big went wrong, a quarter of one of its floors would be a legal apartment owned by me. It was a straightforward risk, like backing a horse. At time of writing, two years later, the race is still being run. The place is not yet habitable and is not owned by me, but things are moving. I wrote about it, soon after 9/11.

For the price of a house in, say, Crumlin, I put a deposit on a space in a warehouse just beside the Holland Tunnel. The idea was that by next year, maybe, the warehouse would be turned into apartments. Whenever I thought of the winter months I might be going to spend there, I imagined walking the lively streets and hurrying in from the sharp, blue-skied cold to companionable meals in restaurants, and then the payoff—being able to do hard work because of being so carefree. Now, I can imagine nothing. My plan, of course, doesn't matter at all in itself. But I mention it because it matters that the gift of hope, which has been Manhattan's gift to millions throughout its existence, and was its gift to me, has been snatched from its grasp. It matters that the spectrum of intangible things I valued Manhattan for, is the very spectrum that has disappeared. The myth that Manhattan had of itself has been murdered. Its harmless obsessions with fashion and celebrity and being where it's at, have been massacred along with everything else. A society that never imagined itself being anything but envied—that could not imagine being hated—must now find dark and uncertain ways of being. I take it that there is dust everywhere on the building I was going to have my space in. There must be dust all over Lower Manhattan. Consider what must be in that dust, since hardly any whole bodies have been found. If ever I look down at a smudge on my hand there, I'll know what I'm looking at . . .

But life has gone on and Manhattan has not been broken. If the apartment ever does exist as such, I do not know what prayer of thanksgiving, what ceremony done in private with myself, what solemn turning of the key could possibly express what owning a place in Manhattan would mean to me. Every one of my mother's family emigrated except for a girl who died of TB. My grandfather was one of fourteen children in a two-room cottage in North Kerry. His father kept the family by walking the eighty miles to Cork with a wooden barrel of butter on his back, selling it, walking back, doing it again. A human beast of burden. What were the children for, however loved, but emigration? Nobody knows how many Irish boys and girls stood at the railings of a ship in New York Harbor and gazed at the land of their salvation rising before them. But I imagine myself, not a stroll away from where their feet touched American soil, waiting for them, further down the chain of time. History describing a parabola—hearth left, hearth arrived at.

"Thousands have lived without love," Auden said, "not one without water." I used to want to quote that to some of the letter writers, even though I personally never feel any better because someone else is feeling worse. But he's right that you can do without the luxuries, but not without the staples. Friendship is a wide base to plant your life on. When I was writing in Manhattan I had a few old friends in Ireland who didn't keep in touch but I knew to be there, and I had Luke, phoning from London where he had settled down with a beautiful Danish man, and I had a wonderful friend who ran a newsstore in Tribeca and the friendly acquaintanceship of some terrific people I met through her. And one Christmas week when I was bowed with depression in the cottage in Clare, my friend Helen came and made me climb a grassy slope and crawl under the barbed wire into an ancient grove of oak and holly, and bring back mossy boughs to the cottage, where we found a piece of old scarlet ribbon to decorate them with, and whether it was her generosity or the raid on nature's riches, I was fine after that.

Art helps you to live just as directly as friendship does. There were times—for instance when I read Tolstoy's "Kreutzer Sonata" and then went up to Carnegie Hall and heard the sonata live—when the paradoxical thing happened to me that my existence was temporarily justified by other people's art and other people's performance.

Those were the kinds of everyday resources I pointed out to unhappy people who wrote to me. Friends, travel, music.

AND THEN THERE ARE animals and birds and pet animals; we humans are not the only living things. Once on a book tour, the dialogue with a particularly lively audience developed into a freewheeling mixture of literary criticism and anecdotes about our pets.

"I've just had an inspiration!" I said to them. "Why don't I invent a new kind of novel that doesn't bother having a plot and characters? Why don't I just go straight to the bits we all like? Why don't I write books that just consist of description after description of sex and romance and dogs and cats?"

"Do it!" they all shouted enthusiastically. "Do it!"

The company of a cat was my care and my delight all through writing *My Dream of You,* and in my own history, both the joy I had of them and the pain—when one died and one wouldn't accept me—are important events. I would readily write about them in fiction, and I illuminated several characters in *My Dream of You* by their relationship to dogs and cats. Yet I never dared answer a letter that was heavy with grief or stiff with loneliness with the advice, Get a dog, or Get a cat. Even though today, for example, I saw a photo of a man waiting to die in a hospice. He was lying on a high, narrow bed, emaciated and with his eyes closed, and his arm hung down so that his hand could rest on the head of his dog, patiently sitting beside him. People who haven't felt it are baffled and even vaguely insulted if you mention the profound consolation that is in the gift of an animal. It is a nonverbal relationship, so only experience of it teaches. For the same reason, while the visual arts have always paid respect to animals and birds, writers who want to be thought serious rarely lower the temperature of the words they use with the simplified vocabulary pet animals bring with them. Yet it is that very simplifying effect that makes a real animal sweeten a harsh life.

The security of money and the pleasure of what it can buy. Friendship. Art. The company of animals. These brought enough joy into my own life to allow me to imagine Kathleen and her resurrection from her own past. But sometimes the loneliness that lay behind letters from strangers was too oceanic a condition to be placed face to face with these small things. That was when I said, Write out your story, if only for yourself, and I had in mind that the slight displacement of experience might open a chink where a cat or a friend or an experience could creep in and take up benign residence. But I always knew that my correspondents didn't want to discipline themselves to writing— they wanted to speak, and to speak to another person. And they wanted that other person to be a person who would listen forever. In our culture, nothing but such a person will do. It has been shouted at us for so long that we're second-rate if we're not in a pair with someone else, that we've come to deeply believe it. One of the cruelest things ever said to me was by someone who meant to be kind: "You are a wonderful woman," he said, "and you've made a lot of yourself. But who knows what you might have been if you'd had someone behind you?" And that's the thing that haunts— the sense that there is more within than you've had a chance to use, and that you could be more alive, more joyous, more adventurous, more talented, more loving, if only there were someone who wanted to bring the whole of you out and see it at play.

But if there is no such person—this is what I wrote as urgently as I could in replies to letters—you have to go on anyway. You can't not live. I used to say, The first thing is that you must live. As long as you are alive, something might change.

THERE IS ONE vast resource more. It is the natural world, of which our troubled selves are so mysteriously the inhabitants.

I walked in Umbria last year from one little honey-colored town to the next—the tour company sends your bag on each day, so all you carry is your map and your water and your sunblock. The first morning I dodged around the misty piazza in Assisi buying water and a cheese roll and an *International Herald Tribune* and I sang as I passed under a medieval gate and struck out for the country, " 'Oh yeah I'll, tell you something, I think you'll understand, when I, say that something, I wanna hold your hand.' " A happy mumble. The rain died away. The first liquid notes came from unseen birds in the groves. The gray track took on light and shadow as the sun reclaimed it. My boots made so little noise on the rain-softened path that bright finches swooped and darted in front of me, and butterflies resting their exotic wings on stones in the sun did not move away. Then another shower. I had a bad time coming down a slope slippery with mud, but being on your own toughens you up. There's no one to wail to. That night, tucking in to asparagus in filo pastry, a stranger might be sorry for me, a woman wearing her years none too lightly and eating alone. But I was exultant inside. I'd got myself down that slope!

The main thing about holidaying alone is the consciousness of being alone, even though each day was full of dog roses and poppies and fat blackbirds singing from the oak woods where the truffle hunters go, and shimmering olive trees, and cats pausing in stone doorways to wash the dew from their faces, and churches with so many life-sized statues that it was as if they were full of people, with angels above their altars leaning down to blow silver trumpets, their puffy little wings holding them safe at even the dizziest angle. I ate every day in a patch of shade, the slices of salami fanned out on waxed paper, the half a rustic loaf sitting on its plastic bag, the knobbly tomatoes on a dock leaf beside the twist of salt I'd taken from the breakfast table, my battered copy of *Jane Eyre* open beside the water bottle. Once a man came putt-putting down the track from the road on a scooter, but he passed, and my frightened pulse wasn't long in calming down. Once, the road crossed a small

meadow where a river revealed itself and widened and became a pool, under a stand of shimmering trees. Everything
around glistened after an afternoon shower. A horse and
her foal were standing in the field, chestnut flank against
chestnut flank. Their long heads moved identically to follow
my progress as I walked along. There was a shed of planks
and wire beside the road and I paused to watch the
guineafowl pick their fastidious way around its dirt floor
like eighteenth-century dancing masters, a claw daintily
raised before each step. An old pink rambling rose covered
the shed. There was a plot of black earth sown with runner
beans on wigwams of canes. In the shelter of one of the
arches of thick foliage, a smoky-gray cat lay, her kitten asleep
on the soft fur of her stomach. I walked away from the
teeming place as slowly as I could. The horse, followed un-
certainly by its foal, accompanied me on its side of the river,
watching me with its great, liquid eyes until it came to trees
and could go no further.

Another day—it must have been Sunday—*crasssh!* an ear-
splitting noise half-lifted me out of my skin as I came off a
field track onto a road. A tuba, surely! That's right—I could
hear the *oompah* of what must be a brass band, getting louder
and louder. And then I saw, coming over the brow of the
white road, a little procession. There must have been a village over the hill, and they must have just come out of a
church, and this must be a special Sunday. It wasn't a pic-

turesque procession or a parade of Fellini grotesques. These were the most ordinary people: a plump boy carrying a crucifix at the front, teenaged girls picking their way along in strappy sandals, mothers in trouser suits pushing buggies. Then the band, about ten of them in white uniforms, tootling away at hymn tunes I've known all my life. A man carried a big picture of the Madonna in a gilded frame, and behind him the priest swished along in his cream robes. And behind him the stragglers—old men in tight best suits. Boys in soccer shorts over jeans. A few old women in black, chanting *Ave Maria*s as best they could given the competition from the band.

The procession got almost as far as where I stood under a poplar tree and then turned and wound its way back up the road and disappeared. And when the people left the landscape and the music died away, I was bereft. I had seen the little community so sturdily and naturally living its life, and I had seen myself, standing in the shade watching it. "You've overdone it," I said to myself as I wiped my face. "You're tired. And you should have brought a cell phone. Five days with no one to talk to is too long."

LET ME JUST SAY that I am not often lonely in country places. In cities I am, like the writers of the letters. Nature doesn't break your heart: other people do. Yet, we cannot live apart from each other in bowers feeding on nectar. We're in this together, this getting through our lives, as the fact that we are word-users shows. I didn't always like the countryside. When I was a child it seemed a dreary, uncomfortable place to me. I longed for the occasional visit to town to see our grandparents when I'd walk around the inner city, eighteenth- and nineteenth-century Dublin, slummy, falling into dereliction, wreathed in smoke. I would have loved to live where there were other children playing on the pavements under streetlights, and people calling to each other from windows. I would have loved to live where there were words written on things—on monuments, posters, the sides of buses. There was a sign in a shoe-mender's window: "The devil wants your souls to ruin, we want your soles to mend." That was the kind of thing I liked.

That—words woken from their habitual somnolence— was what I reached for as my personal instrument of salvation when I started to write. Which is why the Dublin kitchen and the Clare cottage where I wrote *Are You Somebody?*, and the rooms in Manhattan where I wrote the novel, and this little room in Sullivan County, New York State, have been the real fertility sites of my late midlife. Where I wrote, that was where I made my best effort to be a thinking person, able to get older every day without being pulled down by apprehension, looking forward, or regret, looking back. Even the burden laid on me by the letter writers is no burden while I am searching for the words with which to discuss it, because putting it in words passes the burden on, which is why, of course, people wrote to me in the first place.

"Just keep writing," a woman who wrote from Maine advised me simply. She's right; that is what I had best do. Writing, of course, is only a form of communicating. Just keep communicating, I might say back to her and to all the readers who gave me a glimpse of their life situations. We're not different from each other, writer and reader, except in the degree of our commitment to making things out of words. This was something I used to say, when I spoke on book tours, about the thousands of letters I'd got. They were proof to me of our sameness—you could even say that they proved to me that there is such a thing as humankind. I used to ask, What if there is more understanding between people than we ever usually imagine? What if there's a possibility of some sort of cooperation between people everywhere on the planet, since the gross facts of being human—the way we are made of body and spirit and desire to have both cherished, the way we need family, need to be respected, need help to meet the challenge of growing old and dying—are such immense things to have in common? I was a little embarrassed at being such a Pollyanna, particularly in front of cynical Irish audiences—American ones

smiled and nodded enthusiastically, of course, as if all this
could be fixed up tomorrow. But I said these things because
I felt I owed it to the letters—not to any one of them, but
all of them together.

MEANTIME, while we await utopia, we must help each
other as best we can.

What the woman in Maine wrote stays with me:
*My businesswoman daughter is almost always late to pick up her
little girl, and I see the hurt, the insecurity in my granddaughter
while she waits for the mother she worships. And I know all too
well how she feels. But we all try to do our best, to do what we can,
to cope as best we can. I can't believe your parents meant to make
your childhood so horrible. Of course, they didn't. Find a child or
children you can help and love, so that you can be the people who
helped you. And just keep writing, please.*

What else would I do? An image came into my head the
other day. The window I sit at here in the wooden house in
the summer colony is on the second floor, on a level with
the branches of the pine trees. But I began my writing far
down—down where I felt myself to be quite defeated, and
down, when I began *My Dream of You,* physically, in the dark
basement under Hudson Street. But look at me now, up

here in the golden evening light that floods through the windows. Climbing on my own words and the words of other people, the journey has been upward all the way. Writing has brought me up from underground. I've been my own Orpheus.

CHAPTER SIX

The Family

WE USED TO MEET IN THE HOT EVENINGS where one of the village bars had a few chairs around a table across the street, under the dark ilex trees of the public park. The waiter had nothing much in the way of traffic to dodge when he brought my Campari. It was a quiet place, Levanto—a comfortable village grown up where a wooded valley met the blue of the sea. Shoe shops, a market for bright, cheap clothes, ice cream parlors, a railway halt, a few old-fashioned hotels serving dinner at this hour. The young matrons had long since brought their beautiful, fat babies up from the beach, and the pre-dinner rush in the bakery and the cooked food shop was over, and the locals had gone home with their purchases, and what tourists there were, strolling up and down the pedestrian street of creamy stone, had chosen their menus and disappeared into restaurants.

I'd see my sister Grainne and her partner, Derry, coming out of their lodgings down at the end of the park, and more sisters—Deirdre with her husband, Eamon, and Noreen with her partner, Geoff—arriving at the other end, where the track down from their rented apartment arrived at the piazza. My brother Terry and his wife, Trudi, were on their way, I'd know, because they and I had apartments off the same lush garden and I'd seen them locking their door when I jumped on my rented bike to come to the bar. Those two would come into view soon around the corner of the church, showered and brushed for the evening and holding hands, very likely, and talking to each other with interest. A civility never witnessed by my brother in the home he grew up in, I might think to myself. We had just survived our first-ever week together, there where the Ligurian coast rises to a stretch of vineyards and villages and vertiginous pathways above the sea cliffs of the Cinque Terre. Admittedly we stayed in four separate lodgings in the one village, but that kind of territorial avoidance is the least one can expect of seasoned people.

It was something that we were meeting, because we are the remnant of a family who never went on a family holiday, nor even a family outing, not even once, and for whom every shared meal was perilous. Violent, even, if you count getting drunk as a form of violence, or standing up to leave the table while everyone else is still eating. The festive Christmas dinner was particularly tense, because getting that many components ready under pressure made my mother hopelessly nervous and she had a drink very early, and spending a whole day and evening at home made my father feel trapped. But the occasion was not, simply, tense. The same meals that both parents showed they didn't want to share with each other or with us—he ate confections restaurateurs sent in on trays to his office when he was typing his social column at night; she ate by herself and only when she was ravenous—were often surrounded by pleasant little rituals. On Christmas morning whatever number of us there were at the time lined up in reverse order of age, so that the youngest was first, outside the room where the presents were piled under the Christmas tree, and my father opened a bottle of champagne very, very slowly to build up the suspense around the cork going *Pop!* and everyone, even the baby, was given a drop of bubbly to make a toast. And at the meal, each person had to tell a joke. My mother never understood jokes, so there'd be a fond joke about my mother not understanding jokes. But the good humor was a precarious state. My father's deepest instinct was to charm, and there was almost nothing he couldn't make charming, but a lot of the time she would have none of it. She was embittered by the need for plain-speaking. What money did he have? Did he have a mistress? When was he going to do something about whichever of the children was in trouble at the time? Which offended him, of course, and he'd glance at his watch and say sorry, but he had to go—instinctively heading for an audience more appreciative than he got at home. But sometimes, for maybe an hour—an hour at most—our mother and our father would have appeased each other, and she without knowing it had her own gauche charm, more powerful, if less supple, than his. Then, it was a great pleasure for all of us to be together. You could glimpse what we might have been.

Nobody else cares about the minutiae of this long-dead man and woman except my siblings, and they care less than I. I'm the one of them who never had a child. I don't know why—I got tests done in the Radcliffe in Oxford when I was in my twenties and the doctor asked me at the end, when they were letting me go without reaching any conclusion, "Could you have had TB at some stage, do you think, without it being diagnosed?" Indeed I could—one of my sisters nearly died of it. I don't know whether I said to him, or just thought, that you could have had leprosy in my parents' house and no one would have noticed. In any case, I didn't move on through children, the way all but one of the eight siblings did. They disappeared into the families they made themselves for twenty-five years or so. I was outside that common experience and the common challenges of family life that rachet people on, when they rise to them, from youthfulness to maturity. I was in no-woman's-land, here and there with this person or that, until I settled down for many years with Nell. But in middle age, our original family arrived back at the loosely linked condition we'd been in before each of us left home. The three sisters and a brother I'd rounded up for Italy—eight people counting their spouses and companions—had time to spare now, and a bit of money. Their families were reared. Some of them were grandparents. Some of them were retired. Having our first holiday together in our fifties and sixties was an illustration of what seems to me now the wonderful way middle age faces in two directions. We were able to do this because we were getting on in years, so it was an autumnal thing, a harvest. But because it had never happened before and was all fresh and new, it was springlike, too.

I READ ONCE that the children of an alcoholic never have arguments with each other because they're too afraid that starting anything will start everything, and it's true that the nine of us—eight, now, since our brother sat down and drank himself to death—never argue. But things aren't cozy either. The three youngest siblings weren't with us, for instance. I was the instigator of this holiday and it had never even crossed my mind to ask them. The reasons are complicated, but one obvious one is that in a family as long as ours—my mother had thirteen pregnancies—there are different generations. My youngest sister's daughter, for example, is nine, and I was in Italy to celebrate my sixtieth birthday.

I'd said, "Let's go out to dinner," when a couple of the siblings around my age rang me on the actual birthday to congratulate me—"Let's go out to dinner—in Italy!" Amusing myself with the big gesture, you see, just like our father, who wasn't much good at the long haul but was great at treats—in fact, if you asked him for help he whisked you off on a treat, in mute apology for the fact that he wasn't going to help you. But at least he was much the same remote, pleasant, anecdote-telling figure to all of us. I, however, had casually promoted a definition of who's in and who's out, not stopping to think that families where the parents are dead must be about inclusion and exclusion more than they're about anything else. Even though I know what it is like to feel left out—I used to suffer agonies at school, like many a little girl, from the belief that the gangs of popular girls didn't want me. And I know that if I had floated the idea of a week in Italy and the others had all discovered that they somehow couldn't make it, it would have been a bad blow to me. It's one of the many irrationalities of family relationships that though the others may make no practical difference to your life, and you seem not to depend on them for anything, they're bedrock all the same.

Large families, when they have problems, have large

problems, though it doesn't have to be like that—Deirdre and Eamon devoted themselves to their seven children with love and energy, and now that the children are adults there aren't the marks on them of scrabbling for inadequate resources. I remember realizing one day, in Deirdre's crowded house, that the difference between happy children and unhappy ones is very simple: the happy ones are the ones whose parents enjoy things more if their kids are with them. The unhappy ones know that their parents' idea of a good time is getting away from them. The Dickensian warmth and good cheer of the big family is nevertheless a myth. In Levanto, we had a pleasant, mild time with each other. We'd meet in the half-dark at the table under the ilex trees and exchange small talk, both more at ease and more bored than if we'd been with our own friends. I've often been with families or couples so used to each other that they're almost inarticulate—their conversations slump around like sacks. This was my first time to spend aimless hours with my own flesh and blood, and we weren't much more animated.

But I hadn't known how vast the lore is that is shared by even a semi-detached family. Take Trudi's mother, for instance—whom Trudi loved with a delicate respect unknown to us. Trudi's mother wore the same hat from the same shop as our own mother to Trudi's wedding. So, if a hat is mentioned in any circumstances, those hats are nearby. A motorbike might pass our table and someone would say idly,

"How's Rory getting on?" not realizing that the prompt was that Grainne's son Rory had a motorbike accident twenty years ago. Such-and-such a good-looking niece, such-and-such a feckless nephew, such-and-such a brother of a brother-in-law who's bought a Mercedes—immediate total silence, while we simultaneously wonder how he'll make the repayments—at a name, we retrieve much the same data. And when we make comments on little bits of family news, they're based not so much on shared values as on a consensus as to what is serious and what is not, since it's the big things we've always been together for—christenings, marriages, worry over children, funerals. We know far more than we say, like those illiterate peasants who turn out, when the collector of folktales comes from the university, to have the whole of a hundred complex tales in their memories. Their everyday talk must be in the same relation to what they are capable of reciting as our trivial chats in the balmy Italian night air were to what we might have said. There is something rewarding about being in a group that can communicate with minimal effort. Otherwise, what is it that makes family members sit around inconsequentially, as if there's invisible value in being together—as if time spent together doing nothing is virtuous, whereas the same time spent with other people would be a waste?

My sister Deirdre, puffing on her pipe, might launch into a little monologue about how she'd managed to understand enough Italian words to check the time of Mass, and how the flowering bush beside her, when she was trying to sketch the old men playing boccie, had a wonderful scent, and how she'd seen sandals that would be ideal for her daughter because her daughter had lost her sandals but she couldn't remember which laneway the shop had been in, and the rest of us might talk across her, throw our own comments in, offer an anecdote, start off in another direction altogether. Maybe Eamon would say that they'd bought a huge plastic container of wine to bring home to demonstrate to their children how little it cost, and all of us could picture the scene when their family, grandchildren and all, would gather around their kitchen table, glasses at the ready. Maybe Trudi would throw in that she and my brother Terry had gone to Pisa on the train—admiring noises from the rest of us at them figuring out how to do this—and they were walking up the street to the Leaning Tower when who did they bump into but a couple of friends from Dublin! Appreciative noises at life's coincidences. Noreen might have been to the traveling market and seen a bargain in curtaining fabric, and listening, Grainne might unconsciously take on the shrewd, self-forgetful look that women who have brought up families on very little money share the world over. I might inquire of nobody at what point in their lives did the young mothers who spent all day under parasols on the beach turn into the little crones who cruised the fish market? What we said never added up to anything, but because families are usually utilitarian in their dealings with each other, a purely convivial exchange is touched with luxury. At least so it seems to me, though for all I know, it is usual to put your best foot forward in a family, and that is why people rush home to the suburbs every evening. I have not lived in a family since I was a child; I was sent to boarding school the day I turned fourteen, I got out when I was seventeen and a half, and I got my first room of my own when I was eighteen.

After the first few nights it became obvious that some of us only wanted a certain kind of meal, or needed to economize, or basically wanted to drink, not eat, and without anything being said, we stopped having dinner together. None of us ever arranged to spend a whole day with any of the others, either, again without saying anything, and these adjustments were not just amiable but the precondition for amiability. I'd be on the same ferry as Grainne and Derry, maybe, in the morning, as it chugged in and out of the folds of the cliffs and stopped for a few minutes below each village to rock between the landing stage and the fractious waves. But it was taken for granted that I was heading off by myself. I went all the way to the other end of the Bay of Lerici to the hamlet where D. H. Lawrence lived for a while, as if walking between stone houses above a rocky cove would pay homage to him. There was an Internet café there and I checked e-mail, and the ardent girl inside me, who once read Lawrence for the way he made the passions between men and women part of the natural world, went back to sleep again.

In Portovenere I could imagine Byron, dangerous and restless in the tall eighteenth-century houses he and his entourage would have rented near the landing stage, he and Shelley and the women, lying in their muslins and silk robes in half-shuttered parlors, hearing exactly the same noonday chorus of crickets as the Romans heard long before in their seaside villas, and that I could hear now. I explored around Levanto, following sandy tracks to headlands and bumpy gravel paths beside old walls. When you're alone in strange places in hot sun you're always apprehensive, but you have to live with that if you're ever to see anything. I remember an abandoned quarry, for instance, unexpected behind the car park of a supermarket, where the roots of fig trees made complex, earthy caves above the gouged rock, and the floor was matted with grass dried white, and fabulous butterflies floated in the hum and buzz of the hot afternoon. Even when our village closed down for siesta, and people dozed, openmouthed, beside sleeping children wrapped in towels under beach umbrellas, I went up and down the deserted streets on my bicycle.

My days had purpose because I had the others to report to in the evening, even if I made my reports fairly short— only someone who loves you personally tolerates a full account of your experiences. My sisters have been listening to me all my life and vice versa, and there's a limit to how interesting we find each other. Which is one of the reasons, surely—this is exactly the kind of thought that didn't come up in conversation—that it is at least as stifling as it is comforting to be with family. It doesn't allow its members to experiment with themselves. The penalty for being loyally accepted for the whole of your life is that you must stay what you always were. A calm, sardonic family eye rests on the member who tries any little acts or wiles. Reinvention is not possible. You can slightly change the immemorial order of things: you can abjure whatever power and influence you have, for instance, by becoming an alcoholic. Or the reverse: by sheer force of personality Noreen overcame being the youngest of the older ones, and by taking on all kinds of responsibilities, not to mention getting herself from being a penniless single parent living in squats to practicing as a lawyer, became a respected elder. I'm ten years older than she is and I make a lot more noise, yet my opinion wouldn't count as much in an important family decision as hers would. But basically, everything, including the exact weight each person in a family carries, was decided long ago, though by whom no one can ever say.

. . .

I'VE HEARD IT SAID that if one person in a family changes, the others, even though they're in Australia or Timbuktu and don't know about the change, will change too. But I think that's wishful thinking: I don't believe that families are as magically responsive to each other as that, though it would be lovely if they were. Any revelations of mine in the pages of *Are You Somebody?* don't seem to have made much of a difference, if any, to my siblings' attitude to me. We were never one of the respectable families who kept everything hidden behind lace curtains—we couldn't be, with a mother who was indifferent to disgrace and a father who was a celebrity in his little city. The others were accustomed to me popping up here and there in print or on television or radio or giving a lecture, and what's more, I was restraint itself as a public figure compared to Nell, one of the most combative figures in Irish public life. But our family never did discuss anything that might divide us. Some of us, for example, were strongly anti-abortion and some were just as strongly pro-choice but hell would freeze over before the subject was ever discussed. We didn't discuss our brother who drank himself to death. We didn't discuss our nephew who died of a heroin overdose. Our past—those of us in the group in Italy who came from the same family, and to an extent the partners who had joined the family—was collective property, which I had made use of for my own purposes in my memoir. But the family juggernaut rolls forward. It was a few years since *Are You Somebody?* came out and a lot had happened since then that was more important.

Trudi, sometimes, at the end of telling us something, would say hastily, "And for heaven's sake, Nuala, don't put that in a book!" and everyone would laugh.

"How's it going, anyway?" my brother might say. "Still bringing in a few dollars?"

That's as far as it was ever mentioned that I was an autobiographer.

CAN A WHOLE FAMILY be predisposed to deploy the written word, the way another family might play tennis? Or a whole gender—isn't it women, mostly, who use journals to assert the fact of their existence? Or a whole nation? Didn't Ireland form itself around the experience of looking back so as to escape the experience of being unvalued by its colonial masters? Mine is not the only memoir in the family. Grainne has for many years been keeping a journal that is memoir. And Deirdre writes too. She always wrote characteristically humorous sketches based on her childhood and on her domestic experiences, and the occasional one was printed, in the days when newspapers used light material. If we were paragon sisters like the ones in *Little Women,* whose sweetness to each other was something I long brooded about when I read the book, the three accounts would have been generously shared by the three of us. But though we've both read Deirdre's pieces, I haven't seen Grainne's journal. And I literally do not know whether Grainne ever read *Are You Somebody?* She has never mentioned it to me.

There's a lot to be said, in the first place, for her restraint. She is the only other witness to a lot of things in the book and she must have figured that if she and I were to start down the road of "That's how it happened/that's not how it happened," we would never get to the end, and she chose instead to say nothing at all. But one of my other sisters, too, either didn't read the book or didn't want to say anything about it—didn't respond, anyway, to the copy I sent her. Neither did my brother who killed himself—he wrote a self-mocking letter, as a matter of fact, very near the end of his life, saying, "Nuala's book is not for the likes of me." I used to think about those three silences. At the worst, I associated them with what I imagine would be the negative family judgment of me if it was ever put into words— that I'm, if not false, histrionic, and always looking for attention. But for all I know, those sisters just felt I was getting too big for my boots, or they were ashamed of me, or sorry for me, or hurt at the references to themselves, or not all that interested and life rolled on before they could think of something to say.

It was water under the bridge, anyway, by the time we were sitting around in Levanto. By then I'd seen that the silence used to manage things in a family is positive even when it conceals criticism, because its function is political—it is to accommodate difference and keep the show on the road. When my novel came out, the year after Levanto, a different set of siblings didn't comment on it; and the ones who did, didn't seem to notice that it was far more revealing of me than the memoir was. But then, the truth is that siblings, in my experience, aren't all that interested in each other. They can take each other or leave each other alone. It is the stranger who wants to take a magnifying glass to your personality.

When a sibling reads a memoir, the material is in a no-man's-land, too close and also too distant. I think it must be like reading letters you wrote yourself; even if you wrote them just a short while ago they'll already seem written by a near-stranger. There'll be something phoney about them. At the very least they'll strike their author as unpleasantly pert. And if silence comes back to the autobiographer from the family—well, a bit of silence is not much of a punishment, given that even the most reticent writer does make use of other people. There is a breed of reckless American and French autobiographers who balk at no revelation—willing incest with their fathers, multiple addictions, bizarre chemical and psychological and sexual experimentation.

They present themselves as pure individuals, without ties they consider worth acknowledging to family or clan or tribe. They walk away from the people and places they've laid bare. You wouldn't catch them doing the commonplace thing of going from sister to sister in advance of publication as I did, securing what ground I could. Or if they do, it is never mentioned. It is somehow still not admitted that writers are not romantic individuals and never were—that there isn't one of them who doesn't belong to a network with figures in it like aunts and former teachers and less confident siblings and nieces who are ultra-sensitive to reputation. I was able to speak because the family I belong to is a subtle one—you might say that I can speak because they know how to keep silent. And also because I have given none of the usual hostages to fortune: I was as free as I was unattached. But if you ask yourself why there were hardly any revelatory nonfiction accounts of themselves by Irish women before *Are You Somebody?* the answer is, family. That, and place. There's a gnomic utterance much admired in Ireland: "Whatever you say, say nothing."

I WOULD HAVE LIKED to see what Grainne, if she'd been writing for publication, and Deirdre, if she'd been writing for herself, would have said about our parents. Especially, of course, our mother, now that we are almost as old as she was when she died. She was nothing if not consistent. Her great virtue, if you could call it that, was an unsocialized, awkward authenticity that she couldn't compromise, even for her own sake much less anyone else's, so I don't see how accounts of her by her children could vary much. But what I'd fear is that there might not be much about her in any account but mine. I don't think any of the others was as emotional about her as I was and not for a moment do I blame them—she was harder to bear the more you had to do with her. I never heard any of the others use the word "love" about her—nor did she, of course, about them. It may be that they don't believe that I feel as strongly about her as I claim to, because as far as they know, they don't feel that way themselves, and therefore they mistrust everything I present about myself.

The truth is, however, that if anything, I restrain myself about her. I don't expect any sympathy for being hung up on a pitiably selfish Irish housewife with a drink problem. But when we object to the death penalty it is because one life stands for all life. The waste of her life and the waste she made of other lives stands for me for all good things wasted. I was walking across my kitchen in Dublin one evening a couple of years after *Are You Somebody?* came out when I heard from the radio a familiar voice saying, slowly, something that was obviously making her very sad. I stopped, fixed to the spot, when I realized that it was my voice—I mentioned this when I was talking about rhythm. I hadn't known that extracts from *Are You Somebody?* I'd recorded for the national radio station were being broadcast now. I was reading from the chapter where I describe the last bit of my mother's life, when one of the most sorrowful things was that she could still easily be made happy, if you took her out and sat her with a double gin and talked to her and didn't frighten her or reproach her. Even now I recall with pain how girlish on such an occasion her smile could be. I stood listening to the radio. There were five or six sentences I hadn't been able to say in the recording studio at first go. But there was nothing dramatic about the involuntary sobs—it was more like having a bad case of hay fever and knowing that the sneezes would have to be edited out. I didn't even look through the glass at the recording engineer when I broke down. I stopped, got control of myself, went back to the beginning of the sentence, and started again. In public, I was able to get through upsetting passages a little more efficiently each time I read them. In other words, I grew a skin over my wounds first by finding words for them and then by purging the words of their power—by making them utensils in a job, a task. Being used may be what makes the memoirist's family bridle, but use is the key to the therapeutic function of memoir writing. Making use of things makes them ordinary; they're kicked into shape by the time you have them doing what you want.

. . .

ON THE LAST NIGHT of that first Italian vacation, we jumped down at a bus stop in Genoa, laughing and triumphant. "Well! Who'd have thought we'd know how to get a bus!" We climbed up from the street in the smell of hot petrol from the evening traffic honking its way between turn-of-the-century buildings. The scent of tubs of orange blossom took over on the steps and then, in the low room of polished pine, odors of fish and roast meat. Lobsters gestured feebly from a seaweedy tank. Waiters flicked between the damasked tables. The guidebook said that this was one of the best restaurants in Genoa. Frank Sinatra used to eat here, and Pavarotti, and at the door there was a chair, protected from lesser bottoms by a velvet ribbon, on which Pope John Paul apparently sat. Well, we were here now. Us, that had had hard times in our day. We ate and drank as if there was no tomorrow, and at the end my brother orchestrated a surprise—he cued the waiters to start a procession to our table with a cake made of layers of cream and green marzipan and crispy biscuit that he'd ordered earlier that day. People dining smiled at us across candles and sparkling glass. "Happy Birthday, dear Nuala," the others sang to me.

I had felt a small shame at asking the family to go on vacation with me. Shouldn't I have made more of a life for myself? Become one of a circle of golden people who rent islands and villas and yachts and sip aperitifs in expensive sidewalk cafés wearing white linen and whatever sunglasses are cool? But what I see of health and good spirits and prosperity in the children of my parents is more than itself to me—it is an achievement. I admire my brothers and sisters when I see them loving their partners. When I see that they actually like to talk about their children, and that they take their work seriously, and that they smile affectionately when Derry, Grainne's partner, talks about glossy, golden-eyed Hodge who left me for him, and that they do that for me because the old cat matters to me. They had to teach themselves these generosities. I feel that they're brave. If I were to go from face to face around the table conjuring up tragic things that have happened, I'd see a son killed by drug addiction, a child lost for years to a hostile partner, post-natal depression, a nervous breakdown, battles against drinking and smoking and settled misery, illness, a lethal car crash, and who knows what private struggles and defeats. The next generation down from ours is fine, and the one after that— the grandchildren—will be finer still. But for ourselves— Look, we have come through! is what I might say, except that no one in the family would dream of saying anything so embarrassing.

. . .

THE PEOPLE around that table were witnesses to my mother's pathos and her power.

I used to telephone her on my birthday myself—the idea being that the person to thank for having been born is the person who bore you. I'd be hoping, of course, that she'd be sober. If she wasn't sober, she did a thing that even to think of still makes me rage—she hummed tunelessly through her clenched teeth, ostentatiously blocking out the other presence. When her children are together, as in the week in Italy, if she is referred to at all it is as a "character," though not all the whitewash in the world can alter the fact that though she was a true original, unfortunately she was also a mother of nine and it would have been better for us if she'd been ordinary enough to get some ordinary pleasure out of motherhood. Not for anything would I recall to the others a detail like the humming, and the ugliness of it and the depth of aggression in it. But if I had to—if I somehow had to explain myself before a seat of judgment—I could call on them: Isn't it true that when Mammy made that horrible noise she pulled her lips back in a grimace that was the most bitter parody of a smile?

I see any family occasion that's pleasant and affectionate and at which people behave well as a victory over her and over my father, though the extent of his neglect is usually

obscured by her massive misdeeds. The two of them don't
have to have the last word. There we were, after all, like
people in a soft-focus tourist film, wafting back across the
center of Genoa to the hotel after our elegant dinner, across
piazzas with huge fountains, along by the striped cathedral,
through a jumble of medieval alleys, down a curved street of
old palazzi where sweet-smelling blossoms from secret gardens hung black over the walls. We went into a late-night
bar for the very last drink of the holiday. "What'll you have?
A cognac, anyone? Will we stick to wine, or will we try the
liqueurs . . . ?" "To next year!" we raised our glasses. "We'll
do it again! Next year in Italy!" Perhaps we as siblings, now
that we are middle-aged, can sometimes, and imperfectly
but with a true instinct, do my parents' undone work of caring for my parents' children. Why, after all, did I take such
pains with my sisters when I was writing *Are You Somebody?* I
didn't need to. They have to put up with anything I do anyway. It is as if I knew I was drawing a line, intending to start
again, but not without the family, never, however ambiva-
lent some of the relationships there are. I often asked myself during my very lonely times, Who would care if I die?
The answer was: These people would care.

I don't know whether I paid for the drinks or not. If I
did, it matters. Success matters a great deal in the family
pecking order. I'm glad I can say that any musings of mine
on memoir and the family are based on a memoir that was

a great success and was much praised and made money. Everyone understands about the money. That's what much of the validation I took from it is based on—not on writing it or publishing it but on being successful with it. I daren't contemplate what would have become of me if I'd taken all the risks with candor and self-importance I did take in *Are You Somebody?* and seen them fall flat. The humiliation would have been hard to take. What if the poor book had sold only a few hundred copies and got two or three put-down reviews before being forgotten? Yet all the time I was writing it I sincerely believed that that was what the outcome would be, not seeing at all that I was inviting a rejection I might not have survived. Or would I have been all right, no matter what? Surely the self has begun to move toward health when it takes itself seriously enough to tell its story? To tell a story about itself, I should say—not for a minute do I think that my memoir or any memoir is other than a narrative which might have been another narrative, even though it is constructed from profound necessities.

But the family would still have been there, even if I'd devalued their story and mine.

Italy might not have been there for us, or the lobster and the champagne and the cake. But my sisters and brothers would have been there. It is true, however cold a formulation it is, that family is what, when you have to go to it, has to take you in. And for me—and for some of the others—there's more. I certainly believe that for all the gifts I owe to my parents, for which I am daily and sincerely grateful, I am also nearly disabled by damage that happened back there where the family was formed. When I celebrated achieving the age of sixty and being in fine health and in command of resources, I was celebrating in front of the only witnesses that count. These people are the ones who saw with their own eyes that the struggle against the damage our parents did us was long, for many of the nine of us. They know how uncertain it is, even now, that all of us will survive, as our dead brother did not. I don't look on our group, sitting around the café table drinking aperitifs, through rose-colored glasses. The holiday happened on impulse, and if I had thought about it with the respect I'd give the same sort of initiative in another family, it might have taken a different form. Nevertheless, I count that week as precious. It may not have looked as if there was anything precious about it—middle-aged people who've known each other all their lives sucking the lemon slices from their drinks and having a conversation so relaxed it could hardly drag itself off the ground. But if the site of damage is also the site of healing, precious is what it was.

CHAPTER SEVEN

The New World

"AMERICA" WAS ALWAYS THE WORD FOR "promise." America was the opposite of the heaviness of my life as a child in the flat fields north of Dublin, where often there seemed to be nothing to do but trudge to school and then hang around the house being shouted at to go out and play. America was the place every grown-up wanted to go and it was the place from which the best things came. The movies. Parcels of comics. A ruched nylon swimsuit made for a woman shaped differently from any we'd ever seen. I could have told you, once I stayed in a hotel for the first time, that that's what America would feel like.

When I was twelve, I was taken with my sisters, by my father, to a remote part of Ireland, to be left there to learn a little of the Irish language. He was welcome in every hotel in Ireland because of the publicity he could give, and on the

way to Donegal we stopped somewhere for a night. In our
room there were big beds and French doors opening onto
a lawn that sloped down to a flowerbed and a stream. On
the beds there were sheets that were a miracle to me—I
can feel them still, the cool of their whiteness, the glide of
them against skin. His suave self was around the place
somewhere in a good humor and there was no mother
anywhere ruining things. We stripped all the sheets off the
beds and in an outbreak of anarchy pulled them out onto
the grass and played on them there. A summer evening, and
the sheets on the grass. That was all there was to it. And the
corridor to the dining room! Carpets, and tables in niches,
and lamps on the tables that no one even needed! A bathroom with frosted glass panels in the glossy door. Everything was big and spotlessly clean and weightless—not
dragged down. Which were all properties of the word
"America."

I LIVED IN sublets in Manhattan when I was writing *My
Dream of You*. But apart from that, my experience of the
United States has been of hotel room after hotel room, and
my heart lifted every time I walked into one. The continent has represented itself to me as an airport and then a
freeway into a city, past, maybe, a river curving between
granite bluffs, or a rise of meadow with an oxblood barn, or

white homes at the edge of low woods. I'd brush my teeth
in the hotel bathroom, lay out on the bed the jacket to wear
at that night's bookstore appearance, read the room-service
menu so as to think about what to eat, and go out. I'd walk
through desolate downtowns full of boarded-up department stores and along lakefronts and through the tinkling,
terrazzo-shiny environments of shopping malls and past
bus stations where everyone was black. I visited casinos
jammed with housewives playing the slots, and botanic gardens, and small art galleries in Victorian mansions full of
the ticking of clocks. I went up to see the Getty Museum in
Los Angeles on a day of rain drifting across its white hilltop,
and I got a cab out to see the bears waking up in the Mil-
waukee Zoo. I was moved by the footprint of a dinosaur in
the Smithsonian and I bought cosmetics in Dayton and
went to the AIDS memorial garden in Golden Gate Park
and the tarpits of La Brea in Hollywood and the Monet
paintings of a haystack in Chicago and a folk park where
they show you how to make flint arrows beside a river
somewhere near Baltimore. Scott Fitzgerald's birthplace in
Minneapolis and John F. Kennedy's birthplace in Boston
and Hemingway's in Oak Park, a ferry to and fro across the
harbour in Seattle, Faneuil Hall, the San Fernando River,
the Phillips Collection, a Frank Lloyd Wright house,
Nathan's Famous Hot Dog Emporium—there was no place
I could possibly visit that I didn't visit, like Humbert Hum-

bert on the run with Lolita. Not to mention going into
every church I passed, and endless cafés and boutiques. And
department stores; I know the difference between the lin-
gerie they sell in Cincinnati and Beverly Hills and Washington, D.C. Such wonderful days, and then, late, the last
book signed, back to the freedom of the hotel.

THIS PLACE I'm living in, this summer colony in the hin-
terland of the Delaware River, is surrounded by woods of
pine and maple and spruce, and there are wasps' nests in
there in rotten logs that frighten the old dog, and I saw
water snakes in the lake. But it is a domesticated landscape.
And the bungalows themselves are the opposite of a hotel.
They're like a suburb. The dryers are always humming from
the laundry shack. And everyone has to take responsibility—you must divide your garbage, for example, among six
or seven recycling bins. All week the competent mothers
run the show and at the weekend fathers whose business
suits make them look like aliens park at the edge of the trees
and walk with outstretched arms toward their tumbling
children. It isn't what I thought America would be. The
river is; it is wide and shallow and just like the rivers in
Westerns. But this reservation for mothers and children—
no, I never thought of myself in an America like that. I ob-
serve the way the children are both invigilated and indulged

with an intensity my parents would have found literally un-
believable. That anyone could make such a fuss over a few
kids! Yet my mother's attractiveness, in her prime, was the
same kind as many of the women here. They're shapely and
sturdy, if a bit lived-in from having babies, and they have
hair that looks as if it has always been washed in soft rain-
water and combed out in the sun.

This place was founded so that Jews could vacation together, and though it's mixed now, there is still a strong Jewish influence. Last night, a Friday night, a few families
pushed the picnic tables together out on the grass and
sprayed anti-bug stuff around and had a big communal
meal, their candles shining brighter as the dusk gathered. I
was watching from the window up here, and listening—they
were singing songs, but whether in Yiddish or Hebrew I
don't know. That time I stayed in the hotel in Ireland, my
sisters and I were on the way to one of the places idealized
by the founders of independent Ireland who dreamed of
reviving spoken Irish, the way Israel revived Hebrew. Our
native language is spoken still in the most inaccessible parts
of the country, and though the young people born in those
Gaeltacht areas usually want to get out to Boston or Birm-
ingham, the children of Irish townspeople are shipped there
at twelve or thirteen to spend a couple of weeks in a house
where Irish is spoken and to go to classes in Irish and learn
Irish songs and dances. They go willingly, because the

Gaeltacht holiday is a rite of passage in which, away from home for the first time, children buy sweets and chewing gum with their pocket money, gang up on other kids, share bunk beds and giggle half the night, very possibly have their first kiss, and generally, after a day or two of homesickness, have the time of their lives.

As usual, our family wasn't doing it right. The enjoyment began for everybody else on the train or coach, but we were being delivered to the Gaeltacht in Daddy's car—his newspaper's car, rather—driven by Daddy's driver. We were probably traveling in this luxury because he didn't in fact have the cash for train tickets, because he certainly didn't have enough to leave us pocket money. I know, because my first period came a week later, and there I was in north Donegal without any money to buy personal protection, even if I had known what to say. In the house where we were billeted the flock of little girls from Dublin perched in the bathroom a lot of the time, chattering, because speaking English was an offense you would get sent home for and the bathroom was the only place to hide. I couldn't find words to say that I needed time alone in that bathroom—a cold-water bathroom, of course, with a big, unused bath; showers hadn't yet reached Ireland. The cottage was in a green cleft at the base of a hill, and the lane up to it was sunken and lined with thick hedges with meaty leaves, and the trees that sheltered it were sheared by the wind. The woman of the house grew rhubarb and potatoes in a plot of soil as rich as chocolate in front of the house, and she made bread in an iron pot with sods of turf on the lid and she wore a shawl over her pencil-line tailored costume, sent by her daughter in America, when she dressed up to go to Mass. These things thoroughly alienated me, and it is one of the things I sympathize with in children, how hard it is for them to adjust to new tastes and textures. The world is so physical, down there when you're small. I remember Donegal on my body. The discomfort between my legs where I'd folded my spare pair of panties within my panties. The first sight of the sapphire Atlantic waves breaking the length of the miles of Maghararoarty beach, and saying that rolling name to myself. The ache at the bottom of my tummy. The silky feel of sand where it has never been warmed, underneath hedges. The pale, late-night light that came in the windows of the community hall as we wriggled on wooden benches, waiting for it to get dark enough for the man to project the weekly film. And how, when it began, the picture was no more than a ghostly gray thing that grew in definition as night fell outside.

It seems to me appropriate, now, that my body completed itself in such isolation—I didn't tell anyone—and in a premodern world of thatched, whitewashed cottages and stony lanes. My feelings for Ireland are intensely physical; but they're full of emotional mistrust, too. I think of it as a place where femaleness is best approached obliquely.

MANHATTAN WOMEN are so quick and crisp. They move with the lightness of slender, urban bodies. Manhattan women have thrown off the swaddling clothes of the old countries. They don't wear tights—there are no layers of muggy nylon next to their taut skin. A girl of twelve wouldn't be ashamed of the thing that's happening to her. I don't know that they're ashamed of anything in Manhattan.

The woman in a sex shop told me their best-selling vibrator is the waterproof one.

"What's it waterproof for?" I said, bewildered.

"The shower," she said, looking at me as if I were an idiot.

Such efficiency. And I bet they listen to the traffic report while they're giving themselves relief.

In Ireland there are special deals on hotel vacations in the winter for senior citizens. They're called Golden Years holidays. I often try to grasp the fact that I've been eligible for them for the last seven years. In a couple of years I'll qualify for free travel on public transport. Everyone has to have a TV license in Ireland, but it's free once you're in receipt of the old age pension—it is assumed that for an older person, television is a necessity of life. Here in America, they'll go for cosmetic surgery, reconstruct their teeth and bleach them white, exfoliate their skin, tan it, laser their failing eyesight, wear toupees, diet savagely and insert silicone into their bosoms to get a Dolly Parton–like silhouette, get hair transplants, Botox injections, motors inserted in the base of their penises, liposuction, zap their spider veins, attach false fingernails and toenails. There are people out there twenty years older than I looking for romantic action, people who are triumphs of art, craft, and determination. But a pleasant destiny is reserved for the Irish woman when she gets old. She may have been feared while there was the slightest whiff of sexuality about her, but once she's harmless everyone loves her. I don't know whether the man in the Manhattan deli will keep a line waiting, the way I've seen one do in Dublin, while he tenderly serves an old lady one slice of ham. Will the traffic wait while the old lady wavers across the road? Can she wobble off to see her friend, and when she gets bewildered will the cops bring her carefully home?

Once in southern Turkey, stranded in a hot little town where the ceaseless wind blew sand up the streets from the dirty beach and I had nothing left to read, I found a thriller that someone had left behind, all handguns and heavy hints about what beautiful women spies were doing on their knees in front of the hero. A book travels, it meets people.

You never know where it will turn up next. For example, *Are You Somebody?* was read by the editors of a glossy American magazine called *More,* and they asked me to write a piece for them. I am always impressed by the dash of those magazines, though I feel as distant from their world of impeccable makeup and perky attitudes as from the KGB and the spies. *More* is for the mature woman, which I undeniably am, in years anyway. I particularly liked the title: in Ireland, whatever they might call such a magazine, in the unimaginable event of middle-aged Irishwomen having a magazine, the condition of being older than, say, thirty, is thought of as less.

I wrote for *More* about the heart-lightening and back-straightening I called the JFK Effect, the ten or more years that roll off an Irishwoman when her plane touches down in the United States. I wrote about the way one culture— the Irish one—shunts women off into the home as early as possible and the other allows them second chances, even though youth is idolized in American culture and the old men who have most of the power worship it. In practice, I wrote, the woman who cares to keep a gleam in her eye will get an answering gleam in America, or at least she won't be blamed for having the gleam in her eye. I wasn't talking about a personal gleam—I knew very few people in the States and I wasn't interested in any of them. I was expressing feelings of response and release, but they were to the place, Manhattan. A friend in Ireland e-mailed me an exhortation: "Love," it said, "as if no one has ever made you suffer." I considered printing it out, but I didn't bother. Those three winters in Manhattan, not only did it seem to me that I had found a good way, a dignified way, of managing my life without being loved, not only was I not pathetic to myself—except at Christmas—but I felt fortunate beyond anything to be having a romance with the great city.

For one thing, I was learning how to write fiction, though in Ireland I knew I'd never have tried. For another, I had friends. Luke never forgot me for more than a couple of days and kept in touch from London, and there was my new friend who, with her husband, ran a newsshop in Tribeca. Very early on a Sunday morning, when nothing was stirring, I'd walk down the middle of the cobblestones of the streets of SoHo beneath the lacy fire escapes and I'd cross Canal, noting the way, when you see it without traffic, its ancient shutters and wooden cellar doors and uneven roofs make it look like a nineteenth-century bazaar street—in Nizhni Novgorod, maybe, or Manchester. I'd cut over by the precinct house where they keep the police horses out the back. You can peep in the door and see their great haunches and smell their beautiful smell overlaying the smell of hay. Then, round the corner, past the building where young John Kennedy and his wife, Carolyn, lived, where memorial flowers were always propped against the door. At the chic corner café, staff were languidly getting ready for the yuppies and their babies who'd turn up later in correct leisure gear for brunch. Then into my friend's store. She was the central switchboard of a talented set of people—publishers, writers, playwrights, magazine editors, scriptwriters—and through her I knew them too. I remember a couple of evenings in the great places they lived in, and how funny and smart those people were; you don't get cutting-edge New York jobs unless you're way out of the ordinary. The food was always interesting, too. Something like 60 percent of the population of Manhattan are single people and it makes for sophisticated entertainment. That Tribeca scene was almost familyless, the very opposite of suburban Northern Ireland, where the social unit was a neatly dressed married couple, and the wife made scones and wore Marks & Spencer, and the three-piece suite in one beige sitting room was indistinguishable from the three-piece suite in the next.

To actually have a routine Manhattan walk that ended in the newsstore of a friend who cared about the detail of my life, and to be such an insider that I had further errands to run on the journey home, never failed to delight me. I'd tack back uptown with the gleaming shingles of the Chrysler building as my lighthouse. I might get bread and apples in the bakery on Mercer and catfood in Gristede's or maybe go over to Tower Records for a piece of music I'd heard on the classical music station. I had a good radio.

Joseph might phone and tell me in his deep, grandfather voice that I was his little girl. Cobweb the cat often pushed under my elbow and went perfectly to sleep on my lap as I typed. And I'd started at the beginning of Proust again.

I had a proper job at one point, too, if only for a short time, at Glucksman Ireland House, which is a cultural center and a part of NYU. I ran a short course where we read classic Irish memoirs, beginning with *Portrait of the Artist,* and worked on writing fragments of our own memoirs. I used to walk diagonally across Washington Square to the House at the bottom of Fifth Avenue through the winter evening, hardly believing the privilege of where I was and what I was doing, full of relish for the entertainment and insight that would start as soon as I opened the door of the seminar room and greeted the class. The nine amazingly different faces would look up from around the polished table, the first person would begin to read out their assignment, and we'd be off. Listening to what the middle-aged men, especially, wrote was a true learning experience, but everyone in the class was ripe for self-expression. A teacher, however, needs real emotional skill to monitor new writers' sense of their half-known selves. I remembered with renewed admiration the woman whose course I went on back at the Irish Writers' Center when I was trying to start *Are You Somebody?* I used to quote her: "If you were a runner in the starting blocks at the Olympics you wouldn't be waiting for inspiration. You'd have trained. Well, train for writing. Write every day. Don't wait for inspiration." I myself had stopped training—I couldn't concentrate on it because the memoir course was too absorbing. The others were just as involved, and when our six weeks were up they rented a room and tried to go on by themselves, because I had to go back to my own work. I felt certain they would fail—that there is some kind of structural need, in a group playing with such dangerous material, for, if not a teacher, some benign third party, some holder of the ring. My impression is that their gallant attempt did not last. We met long after for a meal and we still mattered to each other, even though there was nothing much to say. We smiled a lot, to express goodwill.

I used to walk back to my room past restaurants where the couples at the tables in the windows were like actors, I thought, so theatrically did they look deep into each other's eyes. They seemed to me to have to labor as hard at twinkling and smiling and talking animatedly as if they were paid by the hour. I wouldn't have swapped my evening for theirs for any money. I was happy with my baked potato and my salads and my couple of glasses of wine. When I did go out, I'd get a secret ache from worrying that the cat would be lonely. I went up to Lincoln Center to the opera very often but in each of my rooms I liked the life so much that I went home at the first intermission if I wasn't enthralled. I remember pitying Nora Joyce once, when I read somewhere that while James Joyce was working on *Finnegans Wake* in their hotel in Paris she went to music shops and listened to operatic arias on the wind-up gramophone—it seemed such an image of unfulfilled yearning. But I wasn't one bit sorry for myself. I thought it was marvelous to have the money to go to the Met the way I used to go to the cinema. I thought everything was marvelous.

IT ALL DISAPPEARED. Well—not everything. Nearly everything. That period in my life of three winter stays in Greenwich Village became a paradise lost. It vanished so completely that now when I think of it, it has no flaw.

I FINISHED *My Dream of You* and it was published in 2001. Almost immediately I started on a second novel, back in the cottage in County Clare. I'd taken an advance for it— with which I bought the little house in Dublin for my alcoholic brother to live in—and I'd signed a contract, and the deadline wasn't far distant. And then I found that I couldn't get my story off the ground. I could only struggle and struggle with it. I was in such despair that I was glad to start my column in *The Irish Times* again, because I could easily spend three days a week messing around with that—anything to

avoid the hard work of drudging at the sullen fiction. They'd
started a magazine supplement with the Saturday edition of
the newspaper, and my column was in that section now instead of the main paper, and the move from the black-on-
white broadsheet to shiny color was a move away from
seriousness. Because of the printing constraints of the advertising that drove the magazine, I had to have my piece in
early, so it couldn't now be really topical. It was surrounded
by "lifestyle" material now, where before it had borrowed
status from being opposite the leader page. It was shorter
than it had been. I liked doing it still, but the feeling that I
had a say in the important conversations of Irish public life
was over.

I didn't have any plans except to keep on trying to write
a second novel. I had no reason to go back to Manhattan.
The space I'd bought in the warehouse near the Holland
Tunnel wasn't working out—there seemed to be finance
problems and permit problems. I was so far away and so
uninformed that I'd decided to put that venture out of my
mind, anyway, if necessary for years, because otherwise the
thought that most of the money I'd ever make in my life was
in jeopardy would gnaw at me.

But then September 11th happened.

There isn't a more pro-American country in the world
than Ireland. In the weeks after the terrorist attacks, a lot of
Irish people went on package tours to New York so as to go

to the World Trade Center site and pay their respects to the dead and missing. My solicitor in County Clare flew there and back in a weekend just to say a prayer at the security fence. I, too, felt a real need to stand with the city, even though there was no one to know, of course, that that was what I felt myself to be doing. I didn't expect the same magic as before. I know that you can't step into the same river twice.

It had got dark before the cab from the airport came over the Triboro Bridge. I hardly looked out at the streets. I checked in to the midtown hotel I'd booked but I didn't unpack or make phone calls or do anything else in the room. I did nothing. After a while I walked over to Second Avenue and ate some Chinese food. Then I went to bed, still holding myself in waiting.

I woke, as you can expect to do with the jetlag from Europe, at five in the morning. It was getting light when I took a cab to as near the World Trade Center as it could go. Down at the end of a block, across barriers, I could see the twisted gray side of a building that might have been a stump of city left after long bombardment. The smell was terrible, down there. It was raining a cold, sleety rain that must have brought odors out of still-warm ash and metal. There was a desolation of mud and great, groaning noises of trucks and machines around the hidden death-site. I stayed there, standing on a corner. The first tourists began to come up from the subway station, leveling their cameras at the scene ahead of them even before they took it in, in self-protection. Then a policewoman told me to move on. It was only when I was walking back uptown and, somewhere near St. Vincent's Hospital, came on a wall plastered with notes and prayers and poems and pleas and contact addresses, with a pile of teddy bears, crucifixes, a beautiful high-heeled shoe, shriveled flowers, a menorah, flickering candles on the sidewalk beneath, that it began to sink in—the way that 9/11 was not war, but an atrocity wreaked on ordinary people. There were photos of babies and children on the wall, as if the dead would come back if only they could be reminded of who loved and needed them. It was a bright, even garish, wall. Death had come like a parody of a festival to decorate the gray street. One thought I stopped at often during the day, as I walked the city looking at shrine after shrine, was how happy the missing looked. No one had ever posed for a photo appropriate to being missing. Ordinary people are photographed when they are rejoicing, and here they were, beaming in tuxedos from behind littered restaurant tables, poised in bathing suits to dive from a jetty, standing proudly behind a bar mitzvah boy, coy in a bridesmaid's satin dress. Every single one of them was smiling.

. . .

THREE MONTHS LATER, at the start of 2002, I was living in a sublet in the West Twenties that was too expensive and too small. I didn't like the area. I suppose becoming an habitué of any city means that its streets lose their charm, and these seemed soured by the hate visited on America, by local tension between poorer people being pushed out by gentrifiers coming in, and by the harshness of winter. Along Eighth Avenue the restaurants and stores were a gay male enclave. In the pharmacy you'd see men collecting large packages of drugs, their HIV maintenance for the month. There was no casual friendliness toward a middle-aged woman. I was cold and uncomfortable and in despair about the novel. The evenings were much, much too long unless I drank, and I didn't want to drink when I was trying to write. I had even lost the ability to sleep and I was relying on pills again. I reverted to the ways of an underprivileged person. My mother, even after years of living on gin and shortbread, would try to find the beads of the right color to go with her blouse, or she'd aim for her lashes with a trembling mascara wand. I made no effort. I didn't care what old clothes I dragged around in or whether my roots needed tinting. I bought cheap clothes and then spilled things on them. I had such a terror of losing money that I constantly lost it. I was nervous around anyone brusque. The news-store in Tribeca had been closed down by its landlord, and the whole lively and smart community it had been the center of dissolved—no part of it was left to me, anyway. My friend who'd run it, even, had disappeared from my life. Without that friend and the other people I'd met through her, I knew hardly anybody. Bad luck sat on me because my spirits were low. One night when I lost my keys I stood outside my door in the dark street and wept. I was sick of myself and the way I always ruined everything. I'd ruined my Manhattan romance by going back once too often. I didn't know by heart a single person's home phone number to call, to look to for consolation. A locksmith got me in the end for three hundred dollars, the poor cat cowering from the sound of the drills. There was one good thing about the place: a firm, high bed that filled the whole bedroom, tucked away at the back of the house above a deserted, wintry garden, and I crawled in there. When I first took the place, I used to think it was an ideal bedroom for lovers who could hardly contain themselves, because it was up just one shallow flight from the street—you wouldn't have to wait for an elevator. Such a flight of fantasy, when I wasn't in line for even a kiss!

One night when I had the treat of a fresh, thick *Irish Times* in my bag I decided to cheer myself up by reading it over a really good dinner, so I got a table in an expensive restaurant, ordered a good half-bottle of wine and lots of nice food, and propped up my paper to read by the discreet candlelight. I hardly noticed everyone shouting "Fire! Fire!" until the water someone threw actually hit me—the candle had set the paper alight. Sadness as farce. I had to eat the whole dinner with nothing to read.

Who could ever have guessed that the journey was about to take a new turn? That the sequence of events that was to bring me to this summer colony was beginning?

GLUCKSMAN IRELAND HOUSE is a friendly place, and I had been allowed to leave some computer accessories in a closet there. But they were changing the place now and a young woman who worked there at the time called to ask me to collect my things, so one dreary January day I walked over to do that, and since she was just about to go to lunch, I went with her. I'd often had a laughing exchange with her about her love life—I looked at her with something like awe, I always told her, because though she was only about thirty she'd already been married twice.

"I have more dates than I can cope with now," she told me over lunch in a student beer joint. "There's a thing you can join called Match.com and you write a description of yourself and guys write descriptions of themselves and the computer matches them up. When I go home tonight I'll log on and there'll be a screenful of messages. I'll just take my pick."

"What kind of description?"

"Well, they give you guidelines. It's called your profile. And you can put in a picture. You get a lot more guys if you put in a picture. And you can look at their pictures . . ."

I was all interest. But not for the obvious reasons. The novel I couldn't write was uppermost in my mind all the time, and I realized that this profile thing could be a great help to me there. If I could get my heroine to write a profile of herself—if I made her log on to something along the lines of Match.com—it would get me over the structural problem of describing her. It would mean I could shortcut all the details about her I'd been trying to sneak in one by one. If she could announce herself through a profile with "I am 21, I have red hair and am interested in antiques" or whatever, it would save me all the trouble of slipping those details in through other people looking at her, her looking at herself in shop windows, her hearing a certain bit of pop music that would date the scene, her putting on items of clothing that would hint at her appearance, and other creaky narrative devices. So when I got back to my laptop, I paid the twenty-dollar fee to register with Match.com and borrowed the profile guidelines and began work on a chapter where my heroine—Mary, she was called at the time—

compiles a detailed profile of herself. She wrote a great one—it took me a couple of days to get it right.

And in real life, I idly posted a profile of myself on Match.com. I really do think it was idle. I wasn't seriously looking for a partner, and certainly not for one who was reduced to using a dating agency, Internet or no Internet—those were for the inadequate, or for adventurers. The reason I think it was a genuinely idle action is because I've looked at my profile, and it is obvious that I was making no effort to sell myself.

What I said was:

Cheerful, shy inside, usually self-sufficient but would love some tenderness. I'm 57, Irish, a bit plump, I love listening and talking, animals, music, food, wine and kissing.

And I didn't send in a photo.

I DIDN'T MEAN those words. I was not fifty-seven, I was sixty-one, as anyone could see. I said "fifty-seven" because I hated being of an age that began with the word "sixty," so since I'd never have to defend the lie or try to get away with it, I'd rather lie. This plump, shy persona was a false one that would never go to a real meeting with a real person. I don't actually believe for one minute that cheerfulness is my main characteristic, and though I am shy, just as almost anyone I have ever met is, I know my shyness is not what is usually meant by the word. I am more than a bit plump—I am very plump. I don't particularly love listening. Loving kissing was a disgracefully coy way of intimating that I had relished sex with the few people I'd really loved. I dashed off these approximations, but I hesitated as to whether to put in the one incontestable fact—that I'm Irish. Irish is a double-edged sword. Lots of people groan at the thought of the Irish, including lots of the Irish.

For whatever reason, there were no replies. None. Match.com probably has hundreds of thousands of subscribers, and you'd think someone would have been interested in me. But, no, not one person was.

And it got worse. The computer kept offering me profiles of men around my age and I looked at them with interest—of course my profile should have read, *Woman writer will do anything to distract herself from task of writing a second novel, including playing with Match.com.* One day I saw an interesting one among all the guys whose hobbies were going to vintage motorbike rallies and whose favorite meals were steak. This one was from a man in Brooklyn who said he was a lawyer who had been an academic sociologist and who was knowledgeable about Italy. He'd studied housing policy in Venice, he mentioned, and I'd just been in the Venice area with the family on our second Italian holiday, and I wanted to know something about the real town behind the tourist façade. He said he was separated and looked after his daughter, aged eight, half the time. The photo showed a balding, bright-eyed man with a wide, sensitive mouth in a heart-shaped face as lively as an elf's. So, though he appeared to be wearing the most terrible Aran cardigan, I sent my profile to this man, whose name was John.

He didn't reply.

That's hitting rock bottom: to have overcome all your inhibitions about electronic dating, and then not even get an answer from the one man you might possibly be persuaded to condescend to talk to.

I KNOW A WOMAN who told me that she was once delivering something to a hotel where a wedding reception was taking place. The guests crossed the foyer in front of her and one of them was a man her glance happened to fall on.

"I'm going to marry him," she more or less heard herself say, knowing nothing at all about him. And she did marry him. I know them and their children.

It is a mystery of exactly the same kind that I did not take no for an answer from the man on Match.com. There are possible lovers everywhere. In Manhattan, you have only to enter your zip code and the kind of encounter you're looking for onto an Internet site and you're told in what bar or café in your area there's someone who wants to meet you at that moment. I know lots of real men in various nooks and crannies of my life and could far more easily than most people know more. I had two or three men friends at the time whose friendship might have developed into something else, given a push. I meet new men every week. If it comes to that, I meet new women every week. I don't think I'm evenly bisexual: until I was forty and met Nell I'd never thought of women as possible partners, whereas I'd been thinking about boys and men since I was thirteen. But I had no difficulty at all in falling in love with her, and I would have been neither surprised nor taken aback if another relationship had been with a woman. In fact, a few days before I started the Match.com stuff I had dinner with a very clever and intriguing woman who'd written to me at *The Irish Times* in Dublin about the possibility of an affair with her, who turned out to be living, of all the streets in the world, one block north of mine in Manhattan.

At the prompting of some frighteningly impeccable instinct, I e-mailed the lawyer in Brooklyn again. I explained that I was a writer, and that this time I wasn't contacting him about a date—forget that—but as someone interested from the point of view of the plot of my novel in his not re-

220

acting to me. Could he tell me please which word or words in my profile had made him not want to respond? And my telephone number was so-and-so.

He called. He said there wasn't much point in mentioning music and animals without specifying which music and which animals, and he didn't know anything at all about Ireland and had never, to be frank, been much interested in it. We talked about dogs—my little Molly, three thousand miles away, entering the situation like an angel. It is my best self that loves Molly. Anyone would want to meet me once Molly gets into the picture.

And we did arrange to meet.

IT SNOWED, you know, on the nineteenth of January 2002 in Manhattan. I'm glad that the weather did something special for us. I absentmindedly watched the dove-gray flurries come past the window in front of the table where I spent all day pecking at the novel. I saw the angular summer chairs below me in the frozen garden become, by the end of the short day, fattened and soft with snow. When I went up to Eighth Avenue to get my velvet top from the cleaners, the lights of the terrace of cafés and shops were especially welcoming because the air was becoming hostile as night fell. Slush slid and spattered on the wide street, and on the sidewalks the ruts of frozen snow hurt my feet even through boots. I was glad to be going out to dinner. I was glad the snow made the city streets exciting again.

I was in a good mood because I'd stuck at work for a satisfying number of hours and made a little progress, and I remember the bounce with which I pushed open the door of the restaurant and swung in. There's something like wartime camaraderie on the first night of a snowfall in a city, and it was easy for John—who I knew, of course, was the man in the coat watching the door—and me, coming in the door in my snowy coat, to say hello with a hug, and it was easy to spend dinner sitting very close to each other in the nearly empty restaurant because we were trying to keep warm. We were sealed in with each other by the icy night. Our words tripped over each other, there were so many things we could talk about. This wasn't one of those dumbstruck, dazed, fated meetings. This was perfectly fluent and ordinary, him calling the waitress back to emphasize that he liked the dark meat of the chicken, me eating too much dessert, as usual. Our hands moved to hold the other's as frankly as children. It was twenty-two years since an evening with someone had awoken so much hope in me—not specific hope for anything I could name, but hope beginning small, like a forest fire, with first this twig, then that one, catching across the tindery ground. He came home with me to the bed above the icy garden, and still everything felt perfectly natural. If we did not wake up together the next morning it was only because Mimmo, John's old dog, was waiting for his nighttime walk in Brooklyn. That's Mimmo, who has been my companion here in the summer colony on the lake while I've been writing this, as the summer that succeeded that winter turns into fall.

THE BOUGHS of the pine trees here, a couple of feet from my window, are full of a life of birds and chipmunks and squirrels. But this kitchen is quiet. The phone on the wall above the table hardly ever rings, and there is no mail or television, and the only human beings I greet are when I go on my bicycle to buy a newspaper, or when a family party trails towels across the shorn meadow below me and are there at the jetty when the dog and I go down to the lake. Sometimes I am surprised by the smell of hot resin from the trees and I lift my head to recall where I am. I listen; no sound. The mothers have called in all the children. I fall into distracted behavior, these writing days. I eat an apple, make tea, check e-mail, go in and try to stroke the sleeping dog so lightly that he will not trouble to whisk his tail. I have a hand mirror on the table and I look in it a lot. The gray is spreading up my hair from the roots.

I know what crucibles do, but I didn't realize until recently what they are—that they themselves are made of earthenware or porcelain and are extremely fragile. Yet they tolerate temperatures so high that ore is roasted in them at an intensity that burns impurities away—calcines them— and what is left behind is metal that's strong and pure. I keep myself going in this wooden house—the children with high, American voices playing outside—by imagining that I'm calcining the waste out of my life. I am trying to refine this story to the least untruthful narrative. But also, in the quiet of these days in the summer colony, I'm thinking all the time—What is the real thing? What is a true-seeing love? Can you want to love, and need to, and yet fail? Can the lover be standing on the other side of the stream with his arms outstretched saying, "Come! Come!" and you not be able to jump? The bedroom windows are open to sighing pine trees. I am the only person in this big wooden house and I am not really here, because my gaze is inward and backward. Except on Friday nights, late. Then, I am as alert as the dog waiting for its master. I watch through the mesh of the window for the lights of John's car wheeling across the trunks of the trees. When I was young I would have done nothing all day but wait for him. Now, I don't stop work until I need to start laying the table. I watch the dozing dog to see when he will intuit that John is near. I wait at the top of the stairs. I hear the screen door swing. He calls up to me. I used to have relationships full of defensive subterfuges, but now—I'm very glad he's here, and I don't hide it, and neither does he hide his gladness from me. When he is here on his own, on every second weekend, we have time to lie in each other's arms, two people who are coming together out of separate histories, and I often believe that we are more than lucky—we are blessed. And I like keeping a fragment of consciousness alive all night, saying a drowsy hello, asking the other to turn over, murmuring sorry for the disturbance of getting up to go to the bathroom, even holding hands for a moment, sometimes.

A woman friend asked back then, at the time of the snow, "But why him? Why him?" Not that she'd met him—she just wanted to know what kind of a person had breached what she assumed were my formidable defenses. I don't want my reasons out in the light. They're secrets as well as reasons, and they'd give away too much about me. As one comes to the end of writing a memoir, after all, one moves into real time. By now I am writing a letter.

I told her that all I could say was that he's a small man, and seems slight and it is only when you are very, very close to him that you discover how much strength and solidity there is to his frame. And similarly, I felt I saw beyond his drawling, absentminded, mock-apologetic manner to the clever, sensitive man behind. In any case, I said, his manner amuses me—it is such an original mixture of American and European—he was born in New York to Austrian/Czech refugees from Hitler, but grew up in Rome where his remarkable mother studied, first, medicine and, then, psychoanalysis. John in no way pushes himself forward—quite the reverse—but it seemed to me that he was both unconfrontational and exceptionally tenacious. I thought his qualities were mine to discover, until I realized that the word "competitive" might have been coined for American law firms and that the people who recruited him for their high-powered firm must have seen through his self-deprecating manner, too.

The day after we met, he crossed town on his way to work to run in and give me flowers. The next day I dashed up in a cab to a coffeebar near his office because he could come out for twenty minutes. That kind of thing. Within a couple of weeks I had to go on a book tour to promote the paperback of *My Dream of You* and he had become someone who would see me off, would know where I was, would leave messages on hotel phones, would wait impatiently for my return. This was my fourth book tour and nothing like this had happened to me before. Which is one of the great things about this time of life—that you can savor good things to their fullest extent, because you know exactly how rare they are. I had protected myself for years in railway stations and airports from seeing people say goodbye wrapped in hugs and tears, and people say hello running forward with joy—those weren't the best places for someone lonely. Now, when I saw John waiting for me I could hardly believe it. The difference between being a person who is never met and a person who is met is immense. They're not the opposite of each other—they're two states with nothing in common. I hadn't known that. And I hadn't known how often people—strangers—would go out of their way to be friendly and funny to people like the two of us holding each other close at arrivals barriers. It must be the combination of gray hair and adolescent shyness.

It is, all the same, true, that I mistrusted myself from the very beginning. Fragments of old love affairs came back to me all the time, like the skeletons of ships sticking out of the water on some coast famous for wrecks. I wondered whether it mattered that in some lights John looked a bit like my father. I wondered whether he'd like me when he knew better what I was really like. I made the most unexpected use yet of my memoir. I gave him a copy of *Are You Somebody?* But don't read that till you read this, I said, giving him a copy of *My Dream of You.* Have you ever known a woman come so well-documented? I said. I never wrote for its own sake, I told him—I wrote so as simply to live, and then so as to live better, and not just to get better at managing life, but to be a better person. I probably beamed at him as these things were said, because I had privately decided that being with him would be not just a help on the way to those goals but part of them, already, amazingly, achieved.

I thought of us as the same age, though when I con-
fessed to the lie I'd told on Match.com, he turned out to be
five years younger than I. When the book tour was over
and I was more often in his house in Brooklyn than my
room in Manhattan, I began to see some of the ways in
which our age influenced things. And not just age, but era.
In his demeanor John is almost quaintly old-fashioned—he
could be a professor of architecture, say, in some charming
European university town. But insofar as that aesthetic ex-
tends to his attitudes, it isn't perhaps the best mix with fem-
inism, to put it as mildly as possible. I've been a feminist
since first I grasped what it is, for all that, as in the case of
Joseph's wife, I have failed over and over again in self-
respect and respect for women and men. Feminists in Ireland are not, shall we say, liked, and the dislike is liberally
articulated in the media, not silenced, as it is in the States,
by the honorable tradition of correctness. The least of the
effects of decades and decades of seeing what you believe in
mocked and insulted is a prickly defensiveness. It isn't easy
to come back into the ways of trust with a man, even just in
talk. My consciousness is so raised that it registered every
time John made a mild criticism of women's matters or of
any woman.

As for mutual criticism, I dished it out to him in huge
quantities, but when he raised the slightest question about
me it was met with what even I see is a difficult mixture of

girlish hurt and adult belligerence. But I felt liberated by
being able to be openly angry and doubtful and critical, and
above all self-critical. I felt that this relationship might have
more chance than any other because my ambivalences about
it, both as myself and as a representative—which is what
feminized women, I think, helplessly feel themselves to
be—were out in the open from the beginning, and he was
constant in his affection in the face of them. I would have
loved to be unselfconscious, but it does not seem possible at
the age I am—nothing could stop my mind from adding its
commentary to every occasion, like the insert of breaking
news that runs along the bottom of the TV screen. And
yet, though all the customs and practices of a romance assume youth and single-mindedness, I did not blowtorch us
with irony. I'm young still, myself, when it comes to romance. I wanted him to buy me a pretty robe and nice lin-
gerie. I didn't want him to know if I took an indigestion
tablet or needed to tweeze a hair from my chin. I once
sulked because he hadn't worried about whether I'd been
caught in a thunderstorm or not. I melted inside one day
when, for something to do with his hands while we were
talking, he combed my hair. When he collected me from
the dentist, I remembered talking in the television interview on the chat show in Ireland where *Are You Somebody?*
was launched about how much I'd love to be collected from
the dentist, and I did love it—I was even proud when he did

it. I saw that these things were essentially imprints about him as provider and protector, though all that makes no sense where there's no nest to build and there are not going to be any fledglings. As far as fact goes, I knew I could protect John as well as he could protect me, but if he had snuggled up to me the way I did to him I'd have considered him not a man at all—even though I've been saying for half my life that what a man is and what a woman is are fictions constructed in the interests of male power. I slid back into the ways of the Fifties because I could feel time's pressure on us. I'm sure that the frank and equal nonsexist partnership that the Sixties discovered is the most sound basis for lasting love, and I hope I would insist on working toward that if we were younger. But I panic when I think how little time we have left in which we'll be physically and mentally agile enough to love each other. In eight years, I'll be in my seventies, though these days I often feel like seventeen. I mean that precisely: sighing and volatile and vague and demanding, just as when I was seventeen.

I felt I could see under John's modest exterior not just an intelligent but an emotionally intelligent interior. I believed that all the rest could be organized around one central thing—that he was someone who had placed tenderness at the center of his affective life where so many men place aggression in one or other of its manifestations. I discovered that though late in life you don't have the early needs—

for a partner, for a house, for someone to help you be coura-
geous—further needs open up, like one mountain range behind the other. I believed that he had a need for warmth
and closeness, and that I had a child's unmet needs, and
that between us a combination of goodwill and experience
and physical delight in each other and wonder at the unex-
pectedness of it all would see us through. In spite of our
poor records. And there was always the backstop—that if we
didn't make it we'd be so old anyway that it would hardly
matter—we'd have more to worry about than the exact temperature of the feelings between us.

He said two things in the first days that impressed me
very much. One was that in both his marriages—and each
had lasted thirteen years—he had loved his wives more as he
went along. "It changes, but it deepens," he said. I believed
that he meant this, even though the marriages failed. The
other was that he had only been unfaithful once. I would
have much preferred that he had never been unfaithful. Fi-
delity is all or nothing, and a chain is only as strong as its
weakest link. Nevertheless, compared to men I have known,
beginning with my father, one extramarital affair isn't too
bad. I could and I did trust Nell completely but as for
men—I'd never had a relationship with a man I could trust.

When we were young we tried to give the impression
that we didn't want the boy we were after, that we could
take him or leave him alone, that any pursuing was on his

side. But I was happy to be open with John about needing him, and about everything. I told him I'd like to find a book of advice on something I had often observed in wives—the art of being affectionately bored, as I expected to be when our relationship settled down. The expectation that I would retrieve my independent self at some point helped when I began discovering our problems, such as the full extent of his commitment to his work. His professional life is by far the main interest in John's life, next to his daughter. Left to himself, he'd allow work to expand to almost all the time available outside her needs. His intellectual life and a great part of his emotional life, day by day, is bound up in the ups and downs of the cases he's involved in and with the life of the office he works in. This cuts us off from each other, even if I learn a bit about the law in the United States over time. His work may come between us, and I also don't know what time will do to my confused attitudes about the money he works to earn. A young woman is often the beneficiary of her husband's work and so forgives the way it dominates his life. But John's money goes and will go to the child's private school and child maintenance and after-school play-groups and the summer colony, which is her holiday place. I don't need it—I have my own money. But I resent him being absent from me, absorbed in earning it for her. And I want to be sure that he would keep me if I asked him to. Yet the converse isn't true. I'd keep him, sure, but I can't bring myself even to imagine taking on his commitments outside his modest expenditure on himself.

In Brooklyn, last thing at night we walk Mimmo around the block and look at the moon and stars. But work, his and mine, and money, his and mine, are two of the big issues that stand in the light when I try to look ahead, though they're not the biggest. Our lives each rest on big, solid, weight-bearing structures that it took long years to put in place. If we'd met when we were young we'd have put them in together. Now, the question is whether making room for each other will weaken or strengthen the structures. In principle, there's no rush. Things have their seasons. Here in the colony we walk down the slope of the hill where the grass is brown now and swim together in the shadowy, serene lake, and the old dog sometimes comes in after a while and his fine head cuts through the water, his cataracted eyes looking for his master. He's lonely at being left behind. Oh, I get lonely too, even nestled in the crook of John's arm, even here in the peace of the pine-scented bedroom.

I wake before him sometimes, startled by the exotic screech of the jays somewhere in the woods. The doubts that live along my nerves start their whisperings. I have taken a wrong turning! This is all a mistake! I feel sourness well up and take its familiar place. My heart fills with conflict and distress and I turn away from him. Oh, what am I doing here, so far from home? "What's wrong, sweetie?" he

murmurs. But I don't know what's wrong, I don't understand what's going on except that into the room, like toxic
gas seeping into air, has just sidled my mother, harbinger of
defeat. My own self goes threadbare as her powerful self
takes over and she, in my mind's eye, at the age I am now,
totters ahead of me up the street in Dublin on the way to
the pub, her back rejecting the home that tried to keep her
in, her arm anxiously clutching the basket that holds her
book, her spectacles, and her money. Never enough money.
My heart twists under the familiar goads of anger and pity.
Her unhappiness seems much more real, still, than my happiness. She wouldn't go out the door without a smear of
makeup, but she bit her nails. I remember the furtive,
driven, sound of it. When I cried out to the psychoanalyst,
"What's that woman doing in America? What's she doing,
following me around?" he smiled, but he said nothing.

I BROKE a vital bond with Ireland recently, when I left my
job. The people who read my *Irish Times* column were my
community—more than that, a family, almost, because my
thoughts and feelings were known to them. But the effects
of the September 11th attack on America spread far and
wide, and one of them was the disappearance of a certain
kind of luxury advertising, and that revealed that our newspaper was in crisis. All of us were asked to do more for our

pay or consider early retirement. I'd felt since 9/11 that a certain kind of confident journalistic commentary looked ridiculous anyway, and I wanted to do something, too, to move toward a new life. So I resigned. But I didn't know how lost I'd be without my anchor of a thousand words a week. I don't know where I'm living. I used to compare them—Ireland's malice against America's sweetness; America's foolishness against Ireland's intelligence. But last night, my eyes open in the pine-scented dark, I changed the question from Which is the better place? to In which place could I be a better self? Which one is most likely to make an unmarried, childless, agnostic woman in late middle age stand up straight and smile and tell the truth? But even as I answer Oh, the United States is!, I think, I don't want to live somewhere that's good for you! I want to live where I know the politicians and where the woman beside me on a bus was at school with my aunt and where people take the trouble to try to talk well and where I can hear my own language, my own music, jokes I understand. Knowing who I am and where I am—that's what would keep me going to my death, not the corner of his good heart this man here can spare, coming back in his ancient pyjamas from checking whether the bedclothes haven't been kicked aside by his daughter in her sleep.

He tucks me in against his chest and he tells me he loves me. He can sleep like that, his chin on my head. I brood there in his arms. I have no relationship with America except the one with him, and no place in it except the half of his bed. Whereas I have something thicker than blood, more intimate than love with Ireland, the actual place, and Ireland the concatenation of past, present, and personal experience. And I didn't live my mother's life; Ireland is a great place for a woman who can live the life of a man, and I lived my father's life. I was a university teacher and then a television producer and then a journalist and I moved around all the time and I knew people it was a privilege and a pleasure to know. For a long time, things never stopped happening—jokes, brilliant gossip, exchanges of ideas, outings, political upsets, experiences of the arts, long, boozy afternoons in pubs with people who enjoyed the display of their own cleverness and charm—afternoons made truly happy if people who could do it lifted up their voices and sang the big traditional songs in the Irish language. I've swum in calm seas in the golden light of a western sunset with complex people made happy as children by the water. I've huddled under the jetties of bone-simple islands while the storm slapped wave after wave against the bucking boat we couldn't board, and run through the howling wind to somewhere where there was a fire and hot whisky and maybe a fiddle or two. I've listened to wonderful talkers and I've talked myself and I've tramped through wet heather for so long that by the time we limped across the flagstones to ask for a drink at the bar, the moon was rising in the navy blue sky at the open door. I've cycled on a spring morning past primroses and violets in turf sparkling with dew beneath low stone walls dividing little green fields. I've sat at my friend's long, polished table in a Georgian dining room while we opened a few more bottles of wine and took the children onto our laps and sang Christmas carols and Elvis numbers. Larks have chuckled and whistled for me day after summer day from a cobalt sky. People have shown me things—the antique wicker shapes of eeleries, the foundations of a medieval mill under long grass, the dates on Jewish graves in a forgotten graveyard, a wooden hall where a few brave socialist women met to try to change things, the Turner watercolors that are displayed only in January when the light is low, how to cook a freshly caught brown trout, the innocent stream at the foot of the tower where Yeats made a poet's home. And the landscape in Irish weather, so full of the movement of rain and wind and restless cloud that when a pet day comes, a perfectly fine day, you hold your breath. And its people—another landscape, a frieze, people in public, people putting themselves at risk for the sake of entertaining others, people drinking so as to feel the happiness of the present moment more intensely. There's a kind of occasion at home that I have never had in America. It is in a pub, not a house, and it is communal, not individual. It builds toward a plateau of utter contentment and then goes, because it must, over the top. The singer slips away, or someone says, How about eating something, or someone, perhaps no longer young, leaves a drink unfinished and says something about heartburn. Or petulance has crept into the proving of some point. Then it is time to go, to peel off, just the smallest bit unsteadily, to sleep the afternoon off.

But then, it has to be remembered, there's the waking up. The dark room and the smell of stale alcohol and no one who has it in them to care that you can hardly make the effort to start again.

MIMMO has an endearing habit. Before he settles down on his blanket for the night, he comes across to stand beside the bed to be petted and have his long gray ears fondled and be told he's a good, good dog. But even with that, I hardly ever settle down to sleep without imagining in as much detail as I can my Molly, whom I have to live without because she's an outdoors dog, and I could never bring her to New York. I picture the little black dog with the white muzzle, running toward me on the grass above the ocean where the wind drives breakers onto a rocky Irish shore. I can nearly feel the wind. Well, I think, I was on the outside looking in for long enough; if I have to pay now for being on the inside looking out, for being offered a home in this generous country in a loving relationship with John, well, I have to pay. But what I don't know is, how long does it take a new place to feel like home? Then I think—Where? Where feels like home? Nowhere in Ireland feels entirely like home, either. That time when I was twelve when we went to the Gaeltacht—our first time away from home—the other little girls sobbed for a day or two before they settled down. But I wasn't any more homesick than usual. I think you can be born homesick. I think you can have a dislocated heart. No place will do. The most wonderful home in the world full of the most love wouldn't be enough for you—you'd keep looking around for where you belong.

CHAPTER EIGHT

After All

IT IS SO STILL TODAY THAT THE WOODED edge of the lake is doubled in the water. All the families departed on Labor Day in a welter of bags and children and bicycles as suddenly as if there'd been an alert. I went out with the dog in the dusk last night and there were two young deer crossing unhurriedly between me and the next house, past the bits of plastic toys on the worn grass, a small scooter and helmet, picnic tables still pushed together. They had hardly waited to reclaim their hillside. They moved off with their delicate rocking-horse motion past the swimming pool where it might be high summer still, because there's nothing to throw a shadow on the white surrounds and the aquamarine surface, though the hot sun is somehow thin. You notice now on the verges how many leaves were brought down by last week's thunderstorm. They were ripped from the branches when they were still strong, so they gleam bright yellow even on the dirt paths. But though fall is not here, summer is over. I see how exhausted the trees and grasses are, and I know how early dusk begins to gather.

I've stayed behind by myself to finish writing this. The time of year is an accident but it feels exactly right. John is coming up from the city to collect me and Mimmo at the weekend, and we'll leave these little rooms mopped and tidy, and then the handyman will come around the colony to turn off the water and close up the houses against the winter snows. The cold will begin to progress down the east side of the United States, advancing through the foliage toward New York in a theatrical blaze. I'll be gone by the time it gets to the city. I'm going to Italy for a week to meet my family—our third Italian holiday—and then I'm going back to Ireland. I'll probably get to West Clare so early that at the farm where Molly lives, my friends will still be asleep, but I know that she'll be sitting out in the lane watching for lions and tigers and tractors. Last time, I caught a glimpse of the little figure before she jumped to her feet, quivering, recognizing the note of the engine. I slowed, and leaned across, and opened the passenger door, and she jumped in, and looked straight ahead, and we proceeded as if we'd seen each other already that morning. This time it'll be cold—it'll be heading into winter in Ireland, too. I couldn't be more aware of the seasons. The contraction of the future as I get older, the narrowing of the tunnel of time, makes each day count more.

I would have said that I was full of tenderness toward little girls. I would have said that if I was lucky enough to meet someone I could love who was ready to love me too, nothing would have made me waste a minute of our precious time. But I know better now. When words became reality and I actually had to live with John's having an eight-year-old daughter, a conflagration that had been smoldering inside me found oxygen on which to feed.

"WHEN WILL YOU be back from Ireland?" John said.
"I don't know," I said.

> "I didn't say one word on Match.com about wanting to meet an eight-year-old girl. I have no interest whatsoever in eight-year-old girls."
> "But, sweetheart . . . What are you so angry about? She's only a little girl—"
> "She is not only a little girl! She's the dominant presence around here and everyone jumps to her commands. She's wailing for her Da-Da before she even wakes up. 'Da-Da Da-Da'—I think I'll go mad if I hear much more of it. She's hanging onto you every minute of the time she's here. Last night when you went up

*to bathe her and read her a story you were away two hours. What
am I supposed to do in the kitchen for two hours? I suppose I'm
the Irish maid, am I? Just fit for leaving in the basement. What
are you doing anyway? What takes you so long—"*

"Now, sweetie, stop that—"

"I will not stop it!"

"Stop it!"

HE LOOKS completely bewildered but I don't care, I won't
console him. What about me, a woman who's lost in the
horrible, hot, lightning-streaked world of jealousy? I am
sick! I want to shout. What about me, I'm sick! I have a
pain!

I thought I came out of the life I described in *Are You
Somebody?* with not much damage—almost none, compared
to a lot of people my age. I have carried a burden of regret,
but it seems to me reasonable that I do—who doesn't regret
good years wasted in a miasma of drink, or staying too long
in destructive relationships? But I never thought there was
anything wrong with me that could do anyone else any
harm. It wasn't as if, since Nell and I parted, I was making
anyone unhappy. Sometimes I said to myself, But isn't that
just because you're not making anyone happy, either? Isn't
that because there isn't in fact anyone around to be made
anything at all? Wasn't the thing with Joseph a total evasion

of a human relationship? What about the seven Christmases and countless other months spent in the cottage
where no one ever calls and you never go out? Wasn't all
that a flight from both happiness and unhappiness? You had
to have territory you could control, even if it meant your
territory was a desert.

> "You're only here for the weekend but you took her to a sing-
> along in that hotel last night and now you're taking her to the
> county fair? The very next day? Does that child not get enough
> treats?"
> "We always go to the fair, she loves it—"
> "Well, I don't love it! I don't love it! What about me? What
> about enquiring what I'd love? I only see you two days a week."
> "But come too! We'd love you to come too—"
> "Don't say 'we' to me!"

Homesick, jealous—it's all the same—me out in the
cold, the people who say "we" in there in the warm.

I'll never be Number One to him. And a child did this
to me! For a mere child to have an effect on my life—the
very thought outrages me. I haven't lived in a house with a
child in it for more than forty years. I never even went on a
holiday with children. When I was in a house party at a villa
in Tuscany once where a sulky ten-year-old took up all the
hostess's time, I didn't like it one bit and I didn't go back.

Of course I knew all my nieces and nephews and I was acceptable to them, as far as I know, as a vaguely nice sort of an aunt, not to be asked anything difficult of, but generous enough. I even looked after my friend's three-year-old girl, my godchild, for a week, once. We got on fine. I'd drive around with her in the back seat and we'd sing, " 'Hit the road, Jack, and don't you come back no more no more no more no more.' " When her mother and father came home and she was so upset that she pretended not to see them and made a big, phoney fuss of me and cut them dead, I loved her and pitied her to bursting point—her hurt, and the way she tried to deploy her little bit of power. But I was more than glad to turn her back to her parents, all the same. And she died, that child. She died of leukemia when she was the age John's daughter is now.

By a child I mean not a baby, I mean a small person. They're nearly always physically beautiful people with minds that startle you. His daughter is. She was laughing up at me from the floor this morning where she'd been introducing the two tiny plastic dogs that belong to her two Polly Pocket dolls. She was sending the dogs skateboarding, for some reason, one of them wearing a tutu. Her face, heart-shaped like her father's, the line of her white cheek, her fine, grubby fingers, her satiny limbs, marked now by the grazes and scratches of a week's holiday—I can't imagine not responding to her beauty and her charm and above all to what,

for all the spoiled American kids' ways, is her true innocence. But to be tied to her all day every day for the rest of
my life, when I didn't even make her! Listening to him wake
her tenderly and their long, mild exchange as she wakes up.
The stuff about school, all the phone calls about soccer
socks and art tables and bathing caps and the endless calls
to other parents. Do these parents know anyone besides
other parents? Do the kids dictate every single thing about
adult life? I mean, after all the playdates and the watching
videos of *Beauty and the Beast* and making them macaroni and
cheese and reading them stories and brushing their teeth
and helping them find the toilet paper—what's there left for
the parents? And maybe that's fine by parents, but why the
hell would it be fine by an outsider, who had nothing whatsoever to do with the decision to have her, who's interested
in having a relationship with a grown man?

*"And every single solitary second of your life is dedicated to her,
even when you're not thinking about her. And I'm old enough to
be her grandmother—her great-grandmother—I'm the one who
has no time, she's only eight, she has a whole life ahead of her,
why should the bit that's left of my life be sacrificed to her? I
couldn't care less where her pencil case is! She has so much stuff she
never knows where anything is. She has toys up in that room she
hasn't even opened! It's obscene, what you spend on her that she
doesn't even want—I've seen her looking around trying to think*

up something to say she wants. 'What, darling?' You should hear
your voice! 'What is it, darling?' All wobbly with loving yourself
for being so indulgent! Have you ever heard your own voice when
you're up there in the bedroom murmuring to her—"

"Nuala! Nuala!"

John's daughter is calling me, smiling up at me in her
generous way, to make the clouds leave my face. She's such
a confident little girl, maybe she'll never writhe like this,
imagining all the women there have been, hot rooms, the
marks on the wall beside the bed, his long fingers on skin—

"What, sweetheart?"

"Sing that again, that song."

And I take her hands and we jog around the kitchen
doing our dance to the song we're learning.

"It's illegal it's immoral or it makes you fat,
It doesn't matter what you might be aiming at,
If it's something you enjoy you may be certain that,
It's illegal it's immoral or it makes you fat!"

I scoop her into my arms. "Have a good day now, d'you
hear?"

She laughs at my American accent and smoothes my
hair back from my face, a gesture so tender she must have

learned it from him, maybe from seeing him doing it to her mother.

"I have to live in Brooklyn to be near her school? Me? Are you kidding? We have to have Christmas the way she always had it or she'll be upset? Tell me you're kidding! You have to take her some-where in the summer for one week of the two you get off or you'd feel bad? You have to or you want to? Oh, you want to. Right. Well, let's get that quite clear. You want to spend a week in Or-lando looking at Mickey Mouse. Did it ever occur to you that that's why you had a child? So you'd never read again or listen to music or go to a talk or have a single interesting thought—so you could be eight, too—"

IF I HAD KNOWN her when she was a baby? But maybe not. The dreariness of having a child cry and cry and not be able to do anything about it . . . Even though late in life I got to love babies when they weren't crying—I even loved them a lot, listening to them exuberantly issuing bulletins in that liquid, oohing, clicking vocabulary that comes just before speech, and practicing the social tones they've picked up— surprise, voluble explanation, command. I wasn't more than seven, so it might have been my brother who's dead now, but I had to dandle some baby up and down the kitchen, up and down, our mother out, not that I blame her. Our childhood was full of her babies—the old pram, the safety pin for holding the nappy closed that was always lost, the bottles that had to be held to their mouths. And furthermore, Your Honor, the only time I was ever pregnant myself was during a very bad part of my life, and I wouldn't have been sure who the father was and there was no competition for the position. I didn't think I wanted a baby, but I didn't think I wanted an abortion either, and one night I was directing a film insert about macrobiotic cookery in the kitchen of a restaurant in Dublin when I felt something hot trickle down my thigh, and that was that. I didn't know what I felt. If anything. There has never been anything as stunning in my life as those three months. It was like trying to come round from a general anaesthetic all the time. It was awful. And the nurses were hostile to me the night of the miscarriage because I wasn't married and I'd had a drink on the way in. The baby was lucky that it didn't get the wreck I was then for a mother. Whatever and whoever it was would be twenty-three.

> "She has always loved anything to do with songs. I get her videos of all the musicals and within a day she knows all the words of all the songs. At eight and a half—it's amazing!"
>
> "I don't care. You want to have a little chat about how wonderful she is, why don't you call her mother?"
>
> "Aw, sweetie . . ."

"You forgot me! You said you'd call me to say good night! But you forgot that I existed. I waited and waited. I went to go to bed by myself and saw the two of you fallen asleep in each other's arms, and Doctor Seuss was on the floor. It makes me sick. It does! It makes me dizzy!"

I'VE RUN OUT into the street like someone on fire from a burning building, even though I can hear his even voice reading the story. I can hear her sleepy questions. But I've run out twice. "Just going for milk!" I called as I slammed the front door the last time and then I thought, "I bet they don't even hear, I bet they don't care," and then I thought, "No, this is stupid. I am not the Little Match Girl. Listen to me. Do you remember all the good times? Do you remember sashaying around Oxford in your miniskirt? Do you remember late at night, half-lying on the floor in some packed hotel lounge in Clare, listening to great singers? What about brilliantly frosty days up in the hills with Molly? You had a great life nearly always, and you are a grandmother-aged woman, well known and liked and secure, with houses—"

But they go to sleep in each other's arms!

THEY HAVE THEIR OWN ways of doing things, the two of them—it has been two years since the mother left, and though her apartment is nearby and the child lives with her half the time, he and his daughter behave when they're together as if they've always been alone, two against the world. They'd be pleased if they knew that the outsider sees the radar screen of each sweep for the other at all times. He takes the corners wide and slow on the country road because she may not be secure, asleep on the back seat. Even asleep she knows what he's doing. "Da-Da!" The imperious tone. He's thinking about her, planning for her all the time. We went to Wal-Mart late at night for shoes for me but they left me in the shoe department and went off and I couldn't find them and when I did he had been buying her thing after thing. A hundred dollars' worth of tops and shorts and jackets. No doubt all the love and caresses and care and playdates and hired help and careful arrangements with her mother and holidays in Disney World and material lavishness and slavish petting from him will save her from falling apart in Wal-Mart when she's sixty-two.

"I told you already, I don't want to look at those photos. I don't want to know who took them. I don't want them under this roof. Do you hear me? I do not want to know what she looked like as a baby. Oh all right—don't bother. I'm going. You're not right for me, anyway. How come the child gets everything and I get nothing? How come you always answer her questions before you an-

*swer mine? I can't, I can't. I don't know how to do this. Sorry! I'm
sorry I took up your time! I'm not worth it—look, you're seeing
the real me now. Didn't I say right at the beginning that once
you saw what I was really like, you'd leave me? Well—leave me,
then! Get it over with! I don't care. You do realize don't you that
it took you nearly two hours of cajoling and reading to get her to
sleep tonight? And I heard you laughing! You were enjoying yourself! What do you mean, what else would you spend time on?
You could talk to me, couldn't you? Is this what my life is going
to be—"*

I BET my parents thought they were great parents, on the
whole. As far as they were concerned, everything that happened to their children just happened. My young brother,
Dermot, was in court when he was fourteen or so and my
father told the judge not to worry—the boy was going to
London to live with his sister. Me! I didn't want him. I
couldn't love him like a mother. What mother, anyway? He
moved up the street into a squat in the end, and the next
time I saw him he'd been arrested at a rock festival for possession of a small amount of dope. He always says that he
had a great time in his teens, but I remember when I found
harder drug stuff beside his bed that I went in despair to the
doctor. "Don't worry!" he said cheerfully. "They stop all that

when they grow up." But Dermot didn't stop all that. I never put his interests before mine, and the only excuse I have is that I wasn't all that careful of my own interests.

Last year I bought him the small place in Dublin with my book money, but he didn't make it over from England until a couple of weeks ago. Now Deirdre has just been on the phone to say he's in a very bad way in the hospital. Two days ago a neighbor smelled gas, and when she went to investigate she found him out in the back yard naked and unconscious on his duvet. They wanted him out, the neighbors did. They kept saying, What if he'd lit a match! But Deirdre said when they heard the hospital did a brain scan and it isn't primarily drink and drugs, that he's got bleeding in his brain, they were lovely and said God bless him and so on. They hadn't known his name, he's so new to the street. The doctors are going to operate in ten days' time. That is, if he doesn't run away out of the High Dependency Unit. I bet if my parents were alive they'd see no link between their drinking and his drinking, or their shipping him off to London and his self-destructiveness, or their shipping him off to me and my panic, now, at having a child in my life again.

I won't think of how much pain there would be if we lost Dermot. And the sorrow for him—that there's no one at all but us to come to his funeral, that he has nothing at all to leave, not a carrier bag's worth of possessions, that he hasn't cared at all whether he lived or died, that—my sister Noreen

said—he knows so little about being cared for that he's offended and suspicious if anyone shows the slightest care for
him. I feel myself hardening toward our parents—going
back with an iron heart to seeing them as murderers.

DON'T THINK I don't want to be finished with all that.
Why don't I smash my way out of that wretched old past
and get out of Ireland and run to America, to the clever,
tender man and make a family with himself and the little
girl? But my hands are tied behind me as tightly as my
brother's are. My brother thinks being an alcoholic is the
most natural thing there is. He loyally lives within alcoholism because that's where he met his mother and where
all their relationship took place. But where am I, if not in
her octopus grip? I didn't even know she was inducting me
into her own resentment of children. And if I had known,
I would have thought it doesn't matter—that I could re-
educate myself anytime. What if I can't? What if I can't lift
this weight off my heart? My breath comes short in fear. I
hate all the women John has ever been with and that's fine,
that's jealousy, that's standard. My mother doesn't even have
to insist on that. But to be so out of true that my inner self,
my truthful self, sickens when I see him comforting his
daughter! To be so marked by what I learned when I was an
infant that I turn away in irritation even at strangers—the

women who summer here, for instance—lavishing anxious love on their offspring. Self-important idiots! I snap. Making work for themselves! Kids don't need all that attention! But for heaven's sake—what's it to me if parents love their children with total abandon? What harm are they doing? What's so wrong with a child getting away with being loved? That's her weight of rage, squatting on me like a toad. And I know that it goes back to her own fierce mother, who never said a kind word, that I ever heard of, to any of her eight, before she died young of tuberculosis.

My brother and I are carrying the Irish sicknesses around. Drink for men. Anger for women.

And pity. We were singing in the back of the car, the child and I, she piled on my lap where I love to hold her, the hot wind rushing through the open windows and the dog's long head under her elbow.

> *"What a day this has been!*
> *What a rare mood I'm in!*
> *Why, it's almost like being in love ..."*

My mother's song. Once, when my older brother and Trudi ran a restaurant with a beer garden, we all went there late at night and switched on the floodlights around the stage, and Mammy got up at the real microphone my

brother switched on and she sang it as a number, with coy
gestures, to us and fifty empty chairs.

> *"And from the way that I feel*
> *When that bell starts to peal,*
> *I could swear I was fallin'..."*

I was going to tell him and the child about that, but then
I thought, "Who cares anymore that I found my mother
heartbreaking? Get some proportion. John's mother's
mother died in Auschwitz."

THIS IS NO WAY to get older. I'm joining the rejects of
the next-to-Last-Judgment. When I look around ... an
old friend is losing his battle against depression. His wife
served us a perfect English roast chicken lunch when I went
to London to see him—she'd made bread sauce, even.
Everything is done in his household to the highest standard. It is full of the fruits of a hardworking, well-paid partnership. But he, who used to rule the roost with his
dynamism, sat there and looked at her with the eyes of an
orphan, wistful and distant. He flies to seaside resorts to
try to get better in the sun, and it is a sorrowful thing to
imagine him moving around those cheerful places with his
pain folded inside him. Another woman I know went mad.

Just went mad one day. There was no one thing. Something in her shattered, like a glass tested to endurance by notes that climbed higher and higher. It was as if the accumulation of pains and losses over the years finally pushed her too far from people and she lost touch with our common ways of behaving. She began to crouch into wariness—you could see it, looking at her. It was the most poignant thing—a mad person's animal fear of the not-mad. Why her? She didn't do anything to deserve it. Other people have bent under as much affliction, not broken. A man I know called to see me at my cottage in the west of Ireland on a rainy summer evening not long ago. Last year when he had a health crisis— something to do with a blood clot—he was rushed to an emergency operation from which he made a rapid and total recovery. The particular thing he had doesn't strike twice, and soon he was home and then back at work as if nothing had happened. He hasn't changed except that he drinks very sparingly now and tries to look after his diet, which is what a lot of other people do in middle age, needing to shed ballast for the rest of the journey.

We had a small glass each of the wine he brought—time was we'd each have drunk a bottle—and walked down the lane to the sea in a rain so ethereal that it seemed to swell the darkening air rather than fall through it. The man was talking pleasantly, but, I began to realize, without the rhythms that signal the speaker is making the effort to interest or amuse the listener. I began to hear how laborious the making of each sentence was for him. It was clear that he just did not have the energy to pretend to pleasure in the human show. There was no point in trying to talk. We came back up the lane in silence. Had that man simply had too big and too lonely a brush with mortality to recover from it? When you get that close, is it then that the silence of the infinite spaces terrifies?

Might these things happen to me? That's what we blatantly want to know as we inch across the minefield toward old age. I don't have depression or alienation, thank God, but I have this condition that could ruin my life. Sourness. Meanness. Begrudging children what they have just because I didn't have it. This summer colony is an arranged paradise for children—the bicycles strewn on the paths, the swings, the swimming pool with its lifeguard, the video films twice a night, the games the adults organize, the soccer and tennis and baseball clinics, the talent competitions and dances, the pancake breakfasts that parents buy their kids in the diner down in the village. When my sisters and I were children, there was a ditch—muddy, ferny, a trickle of clear water over its stony bed—that went under the road near where we lived. When you climbed down and peered along it, you could see daylight on the other side, and we conferred magic on the dark stretch in between. The Secret, we called the place. Once, a visitor gave us a whole block of ice cream and it was such a treasure that we hid it in the ditch and came back the next day for it, not realizing that it would melt. This was when we lived in the country, before electricity came to our house, and when we knew very little about the world. I do not say our way of having things and imagining things was better or worse than what I see around me here. Last weekend John's daughter and two other beautiful little girls played in the bedroom at giving each other manicures, and then they took their dolls to the beach, which was the square of rug beside her bed. They did a lot of solemn inquiring of each other whether they should wear their jewelry into the waves.

Through the screens I can hear children now, playing on the tarmac square above the lake. They have high, chipmunk voices, and one of them is a bossy little girl of maybe four years old who is organizing two relatively laconic little boys. The way they all love to use their lungs to scream unheeded orders at each other! Their bodies are beautiful, but what I love most is the more elusive spirit in action. Sometimes John's daughter becomes completely engrossed in some thought or action, and falls away into her inner self as if other people no longer existed, and then—for reasons she never shares—she comes back and starts demanding a dialogue with her father again.

The children I am listening to—their confident voices will become darkened and inflected by the business of liv-

ing. Look what we all have to accept! A tiny arc of existence.
A certainty of self-importance in the face of complete help-
lessness about birth and temperament and life chances and
accident and illness and death. I take the little girl on my
knee. We have a disgraceful conversation about the different kinds of poop Mimmo does, pealing with giggles.

I'D NEVER BEEN to a therapist before, but how could I
not go now, when I had to swallow my bile if John carried
his child downstairs? Desolate and angry, time after time.
And Saturdays I have to prepare for because that's the night
he lies on the quilt and holds her till she goes to sleep.

"It's wrong!" I shout at him.

"Why's it wrong?" John says with his usual mildness.
"We did that when she was a baby—"

"I don't care! It's wrong! She's nearly a woman! Don't say
'we' to me—"

OFTEN, SHE PEEKS from over his shoulder with a tentative smile—touchingly ready for a bit of fun. But however
much fun we have, she runs back into his arms. "What is it,
sweetie?" he murmurs, kissing her glossy black hair. In his
special voice for her, he says it. Where can I turn? These
things coming up out of me are so powerful. They're pow-

erful beyond what intelligence or humor or the dictates of self-interest can control, so they must come from far beneath the level of reason. And what is there besides psychoanalysis that offers to heal at that level? The rite of exorcism?

"Is 'jealousy' the right word for it, do you think?" the analyst said.

"Anger?"

"Anger passes."

"I suppose you want me to say envy."

"What do you think envy is?"

"A settled state," I said. "Not volatile, like jealousy. And full of desire as well as hate—wanting what it hates."

WHEN I WROTE *Are You Somebody?* I ended it on a path above the Atlantic where the dog and I sat alone one Christmas Day as a still, frosty evening drew in. Behind us rose the limestone landscape of the Burren, and in front the subtle shapes of the Aran Islands lay on the turquoise sea. Beyond them, three thousand miles of ocean rolled between me and America. "In front of me," I wrote, in the last few words of autobiography I ever thought I'd write, "there is a vista: empty, but inexpressibly spacious. Between those two—landscape of stone and wide blue air—is where I am." Now, at the other end of six years and on the other

side of that three thousand miles, I see how vague a vision
that was, and how little there was in it to sustain me. Time
had no presence there. And where are other people? What
good are stone and air to me now, in the real world? I want
to be able to be glad when the child runs into our bed. I
want to say to him that I've a plan for her and me to learn
some poems together—American ones and Irish ones and
English ones. I want to go back to central Europe, to Hungary and Bohemia, to all the little towns where his ancestors
were rabbis and factory owners, when she's of an age to go,
in a good car—he's a wonderful driver—him, her, and me.

But I lose heart. I said to him a few days ago, when I had
slammed doors and yelled at the two of them and soured
the happy atmosphere of the day:

"I tell you what I could do. I could go back to Ireland
now and maybe come back in a few years."

"A few years?"

"She'd be older. I might do it better . . ."

But even as I said it I knew that you can't say things like
that at this time of life. There aren't the years to play with.

WHAT DOES that mother of mine want me to do, anyway? End up like her? She died sometime in her late sixties—she kept her precise age vague. She never claimed her
free travel pass. There wasn't anywhere she wanted to travel

to, and she wouldn't have wanted her photograph taken for the pass, either, even though, in spite of eating only a few pathetic things—shortbread biscuits, porridge, cocoa—she could look beautiful. Her skin and teeth and hair still had something of the glow she had in snapshots as a girl at the seaside. It took stubborn determination on her part to get death to come for what had been so sturdy. She had to prepare for it by setting up the terrible boredom she lived in. No one mattered, now my father was gone, and he didn't matter either, because he was gone. There were two or three of her children she was pleased enough to see, but only if they didn't interfere with wherever she was in her daily effort to get out of consciousness. The people she'd been drinking with in the same pub for more than twenty years were dying off, and the ones left could hardly work up the energy to greet each other. A lot of Irish pubs are like that— they've a hardcore of regulars so dead to themselves and each other that they might as well be those ancestor effigies the tribes in Papua prop along the ridges of jungle cliffs.

I see how it is when people get tired of life. Women seem to dessicate, and men to get lazy. They narrow everything down to what they can handle without effort—the family, the fellows at work, the little circle of companions— and they allow the flesh to fall out over their waistbands and the rest of their bodies to go flaccid, too. Their bodies say that they acquiesce in the common fate. But I watch what's happening to me as if it's happening to someone else. The skin under my mother's upper arm did not become a flap, as mine has done, and her throat did not go sinewy, and weight did not settle like a tyre between her hips, lending her walk a hint of waddle. She didn't even go gray. Every so often when she was in a worse state than usual, maybe passing out in the street, or vomiting in public, or lying on her bed groaning in pain, my elder sister would somehow get her into a clinic to dry out, and she accepted the regimen there with the submission to authority that was an aspect of the childishness that also kept her young. A primitive vanity would revive. She'd ask one of us to get her cream to do the hair on her legs—her hands were fairly steady now—and a box of something called Heavenly Harmony, a coloring shampoo. She was as near perfectly self-destructive as a person can be, yet she caught her hair every time before it outgrew that chestnut tint. One of the things I could do to shake her off would be to let my hair go gray. John asked for that—he said he'd love it. He kissed the gray bit at the temple, under my blond highlights. Sometimes I think I could love him forever.

The climb toward that love, which includes loving his child, may not be impossible. I think there might already have been something too small to call a move. I remember looking at a field of burnished, golden corn on a still, hot day—I suppose in Umbria somewhere—and wondering how I knew that a secret rustle was running through it, since the stalks did not move. Like that.

"How would you describe how you felt about your father?" the analyst said.

"Well," I answered very hesitantly, "I *liked* him. I was interested in him . . ."

"How would you describe how he felt about you?"

"Well"—even more hesitantly—"he liked me, too. Or, he did sometimes. Or, he did when I was grown up . . ."

There was a packet of old letters I could look at again. I cycled home as fast as I could—well, John's home, not necessarily my home at all. Down a street of handsome brownstones, a glimpse of the exotic blue of New York Harbor, across the harsh black and white of the industrial landscape around the Gowanus Canal, then up through the dapple of leafy sunlight into the cool of the house. I let the dog and the cat out into the garden but I don't like going out there myself. He got married out there.

The letters had been in the locked trunk I split open when I began to write *Are You Somebody?* They were written from England when I was twenty-one to my then lover, who must have returned them. I had them with me to maybe use as research material about the Sixties for the novel I was writing. Now I spread them out on the kitchen table and found a red marker in the child's toybox, to number the pages. There were three mentions of my father.

One:

Daddy rang me last night and asked had I a few shillings and of course I hadn't but I never can ask him.

Two:

I think even Daddy is surprised at my virulent reaction to this place, he sounded even a bit worried on the phone. I'm sure that if I hid nothing when I came home and explained how dreadful it is and cried, they would not make me come back. Once he made me go to a shorthand-typing school in spite of all my logical objections and I sulked and was bitter but he still made me go but one day I came home for lunch just too fed up and wept and wept and that touched his stony heart and he said "it's all right, chicken, you needn't go back."

Three:

I forgot to give you back the money you'd given me when Daddy gave me more.

I thought he didn't do things like that—phoning me, giving me money. I always thought that he didn't reach across my mother to care for us. The dynamic was between them, as I remember, he both extraordinarily accepting of her and unkind in a number of chilly, elegant ways, and she going her own willful, drunk way. So. What about the fatherliness in these three mentions? It doesn't add up to very much, compared to the nonstop, total father's love I find myself trying to live beside at the moment. But it's better than nothing. And in any case, it's all I've got.

BUT THE REALLY HOPEFUL THING is—I see those clues now, and I didn't six years ago when I last looked at the letters. Is it that I see evidence differently breathing American rather than Irish air? Or can it be that John's love for his child wakened the memory of fatherly love in me?

I said to the analyst, "Maybe my father did love me."

"You said he liked you," the analyst said. "Now you're saying he may have loved you. There's all the difference in the world between those two things."

THAT'S ALL. That's the infinitesimal rustle in the cornfield.

I STOOD in the shower just now, to get cool again. It's so hot that even the delicate little finches that usually flit among the pine branches have disappeared. Everything except the crickets has been slowed and silenced. I checked that Mimmo was still breathing where he lies on his side, his front legs stretched as neatly in front of him as if he had arranged them to show that he's a good boy. I laid my head gently to his floppy gray ear. I'm afraid he'll die because he's old and gets seizures, but the heat has simply felled him. It's terribly humid here. The newspaper says it's torrid in the city. Here, apparently, is more sultry than torrid. In Ireland, you wouldn't hear either word used about weather in a lifetime. About striptease, more likely. Last night I walked the dog along the track beside the woods under a few stars dulled by the fuzziness of a hot sky that flickered with an unsteady radiance that came and went. Sheet lightning. The air tonight feels as foreign as in really foreign places—Dakar, Manila. The bedroom has low windows almost touched by the trees, but there is no cool draft anywhere, and the houses in this colony are for summer use only and their old wiring doesn't support air conditioning. Last weekend John was here on his own. The hair on his shoulders was in whorls with sweat. Our bodies were too slippery for love. We rolled apart to get away from the warmth of the other body. Even at dawn, when he got up to drive back to Manhattan to start the week of work, it was too uncomfortable on the bed to allow him to pull the sheet over me.

MY HANDS in front of me on the keyboard are veined and
freckled. I am aware of my physical being all the more intensely because all I do is write. There's the complex feel of
my body—the curve of my belly against my thighs, my bare
feet on the wood of the floor, the slight ache in my buttocks
from long hours sitting on this wooden chair, the tension in
my right hand from holding it, hollowed, over the laptop's
mouse. There's the hot, still air on my skin. All summer
there were the noises of children running and laughing between bikes and swings out there, and when the last of their
calls died away, after nightfall, there was sometimes in the
silence the approaching whisper of a heavy shower of rain.
It is raining now. That means that in the morning when the
dog and I go down the grassy slope to the lake, my canvas
shoes will squelch with wet even before I get wet myself. I
think I will remember forever the feel of the wooden dock
here—how it tilts slightly forward as I walk out along it,
how the cold water slides across the warm planks. I slip in,
trying not to disturb the sheen of the water. The ducks pad-
dle calmly past my nose. The dog is crouched above the
bushes on the shore, fascinated by the traffic of bees. I go
back up to the apartment and shower, and walk between
one small room and another, putting on a kettle for tea,
looking around for a comb, hitting a key on the laptop to

light the screen so as to frown over the last few sentences
I've written, matching them against their ideal shape in my
head. There's one CD I play a lot, of cello and piano sonatas
by Beethoven. Sometimes I'm the cello and sometimes the
piano. The big refrigerator whines. You can open its door
for a moment to get a waft of cool.

Oh, let me have a long time yet in this beautiful world
and let him stay by me and not get tired of my difficulties!
I rang up the Central Statistics Office in Dublin. Yes, sta-
tistically, an Irishwoman who is my age now will live to
seventy-eight and three quarters. That gives me sixteen and
a half years. By then maybe I'll be willing to die. It depends,
I suppose, on who has gone before. A child does leave a
playground, however reluctantly, when all the friends he's
been playing with have gone home. There's been a first
warning, for our generation. Our sister-in-law Trudi has
been a friend of the family for the last thirty-five years. This
year she was told she had cancer. She did a course of
chemotherapy first, then they operated, then she got an in-
fection in hospital and ended up in intensive care for a long
time, and when I saw her after that, she was as frail as an old,
old woman. Yet it seems that she'll be with us in Italy soon
on our third family holiday, her hair grown back a pale fur,
herself and my brother holding hands, the most genial couple of all. John will be with me if all goes well. I know my sisters will ask him about his child very warmly. Give me the

grace not to say anything sour, to watch his face brighten at the chance of talking about her, and not cut him off! Luke and his lover are booked to stay in the same village. If it all happens, if Trudi continues to improve, if our young brother is recovering from surgery in some caring place and for once we know where he is and that he's all right, if nothing else has gone wrong, if John still loves me—if some evening we sit around some table high above the sea, the twelve of us, then that will be the moment in my life nearest to having everything. I know perfectly well that in real life I don't even help out by collecting John's child from school. But if I achieve a chosen family, if I have it around me even only once, mightn't that make the enraged eight-year-old inside me slink away at last, leaving room for the real eight-year-old?

TRUDI HAD TO WAIT after surgery to be told whether she still had cancer or not. I called her from America during that time and that was when I told her—because in the family it was big news—that I had found someone I believed I could love but there were problems, that he'd been married twice before and shared the child with the wife, and I didn't like—

"Oh, *go for it,* Nuala," her exhausted voice suddenly got

strong enough to urge. "Oh, if I'd known!" she said. "I see it now, Nuala—don't waste your life, seize the day, *go for it!*"

My Australian friend who lives in New York said to me, "My children are Americans. Everything is reversed. My children are my roots."

Could this child of another mother be that for me? Could such a gift have come my way? That through her and her father, tendrils of a new life could reach out, in this American soil, and growth could start again? Why isn't that just as likely as anything else? The truth is that my life has always been a mixture—I have sunk low, but I hung on; I do get lost, but I find my way back. I plainly do know things even though I think I don't. If I go back to the beginning of the six years that I've written about here, I did know that Nell and I should part, and I did know not to run away from Luke's friendship even though it threatened me, and I did know to sit down and write *Are You Somebody?* once I got a chance. Can't I go on somehow getting the big things right? When he comes out of her room after kissing her with a warm, smacking kiss and turning off the light, can't I say like a fond mother, "Did she enjoy the new story?" Or just smile, for heaven's sake. No big deal. I only have to survive, after all. I don't have to be Superwoman.

Let me be Jane Eyre, prim and tough, and in the end, adored by father and child, and not the lunatic woman, cackling madly up in the attic. Of all things I would ask of life now, the thing I want most is to learn ordinary, daily love. If I could love more steadily than I ever thought I could—more than I ever saw done—I know I would be saved. And then—I would have very much to give. I could make that child laugh. I could be the other half of his love for her. As it is, sometimes when I catch sight of her I have to stop myself from moving toward her. What that impulse is I do not know. It is not pity, though I sometimes do pity her. I look at her through the arch from the kitchen in the house in Brooklyn, sitting on the couch in the next room, watching a video, or drawing, or talking or singing to her dolls and herself. I know how much we all need each other's protection. It was never she herself that troubled me. Not loving her is not due to her not being lovable, though of course she is a pain in the neck sometimes. Huge bolts of lightning that she does not see collect around her, and her small self is the rod.

MAYBE I'M CLIMBING toward the light all the time though I don't know it. I said on the last page of *Are You Somebody?* that I had come to see my parents as not very good and not very bad but a mixture, like myself, and I said that

I forgave them. But I wonder, was that reconciliation forced on me by the fact that the book was ending? Today, it seems to me that there is no closing of the account with parents. I may be beginning to settle with my father, but I think I will be haunted by my mother forever. It gives me hope, all the same, that I'm not sure anymore that the best thing to do with her is forgive her. There's more at stake now than ever before, and it is much, much later in life. Why not steel myself to split up with her this time? Tell her to manage by herself at last?

"Listen!" I could say to her, and she'd lift her head from where she's reading her book on a high stool at the bar, one shaky white hand resting on the base of her glass for reassurance. "Listen!" And just as she moves to make room for me to get up on the stool beside hers, just as she gestures to the barman to get me a drink, I'd say, "Goodbye," and even though I'd never forgive myself, I'd turn my back on her and walk out the door.

ABOUT THE AUTHOR

Nuala O'Faolain is the author of *Are You Somebody?*, a memoir, and *My Dream of You*, a novel. She lives in the west of Ireland and in New York City and is working on her second novel.